Superior Customer Satisfaction and Loyalty

Also available from ASQ Quality Press:

Beyond the Ultimate Question: A Systematic Approach to Improve Customer Loyalty
Bob E. Hayes

Measuring Customer Satisfaction and Loyalty: Survey Design, Use, and Statistical Analysis Methods, Third Edition
Bob E. Hayes

Managing the Customer Experience: A Measurement-Based Approach
Morris Wilburn

Customer Satisfaction Research Management
Derek Allen

Competing for Customers and Winning with Value: Breakthrough Strategies for Market Dominance
R. Eric Reidenbach and Reginald W. Goeke

Analysis of Customer Satisfaction Data
Derek Allen and Tanniru R. Rao

Six Sigma Marketing: From Cutting Costs to Growing Market Share
R. Eric Reidenbach

ANSI/ISO/ASQ Q10002-2004: Quality management — Customer satisfaction — Guidelines for complaints handling in organizations
ANSI/ISO/ASQ

The Certified Manager of Quality/Organizational Excellence Handbook, Third Edition
Russell T. Westcott, editor

The Quality Toolbox, Second Edition
Nancy R. Tague

Making Change Work: Practical Tools for Overcoming Human Resistance to Change
Brien Palmer

Innovation Generation: Creating an Innovation Process and an Innovative Culture
Peter Merrill

To request a complimentary catalog of ASQ Quality Press publications, call 800-248-1946, or visit our Web site at http://qualitypress.asq.org.

Superior Customer Satisfaction and Loyalty

Engaging Customers to
Drive Performance

Sheldon D. Goldstein

ASQ Quality Press
Milwaukee, Wisconsin

American Society for Quality, Quality Press, Milwaukee, WI 53203
© 2010 by ASQ
All rights reserved. Published 2009.
Printed in the United States of America.

15 14 13 12 11 10 09   5 4 3 2 1

Library of Congress Cataloging-in-Publication Data

Goldstein, Sheldon D.
Superior customer satisfaction and loyalty : engaging customers to drive performance / Sheldon D. Goldstein.
   p. cm.
Includes index.
ISBN 978-0-87389-775-4 (hc)
1. Consumer satisfaction. 2. Customer loyalty. 3. Customer relations. I. Title.

HF5415.335.G65 2009
658.8'12—dc22
                           2009028328

No part of this book may be reproduced in any form or by any means, electronic, mechanical, photocopying, recording, or otherwise, without the prior written permission of the publisher.

Publisher: William A. Tony
Acquisitions Editor: Matt T. Meinholz
Project Editor: Paul O'Mara
Production Administrator: Randall Benson

ASQ Mission: The American Society for Quality advances individual, organizational, and community excellence worldwide through learning, quality improvement, and knowledge exchange.

Attention Bookstores, Wholesalers, Schools, and Corporations: ASQ Quality Press books, videotapes, audiotapes, and software are available at quantity discounts with bulk purchases for business, educational, or instructional use. For information, please contact ASQ Quality Press at 800-248-1946, or write to ASQ Quality Press, P.O. Box 3005, Milwaukee, WI 53201-3005.

To place orders or to request a free copy of the ASQ Quality Press Publications Catalog, including ASQ membership information, call 800-248-1946. Visit our Web site at www.asq.org or http://www.asq.org/quality-press.

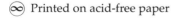 Printed on acid-free paper

Quality Press
600 N. Plankinton Avenue
Milwaukee, Wisconsin 53203
Call toll free 800-248-1946
Fax 414-272-1734
www.asq.org
http://www.asq.org/quality-press
http://standardsgroup.asq.org
E-mail: authors@asq.org

Dedication

This book is dedicated to my wonderful wife Lori, my perfect match.

Contents

List of Figures and Tables ix

Preface xi

Chapter 1   Introduction 1

Chapter 2   Ask Your Customers What They Want 5
   Gathering Data and Using Rating Scales 8
   The Importance of Each Customer-Identified Attribute 16
   Benchmarking 18
   Creating the Equity Curve 20

Chapter 3   Customer Feedback and Satisfaction Metrics 25
   Analyzing the Data (Descriptive Statistics) 34
   Ordinal Data Metrics 35
   Which Attributes Differ From the Others? 42

Chapter 4   Comparing the Data (Rank Order Analysis) 47

Chapter 5   Methods Used to Find Underlying Causes 61
   Systems versus Underlying Causes 61
   The Plan, Do, Study, Act Cycle 64
   Do the Areas Needing Improvement Play to
      Our Strengths? 72
   Overcoming Resistance to Change 75

**Chapter 6   Setting Improvement Objectives and
          Customer Satisfaction Goals** 83
   Making It Happen Takes a High-Level Champion 88

Chapter 7 Implementation 93
    Step 1: Put a Plan on Paper 93
    Step 2: Empower the Action Team with Full Authority 97

Chapter 8 Sustaining the Improvements 103

Postscript *119*
Index *121*

List of Figures and Tables

Figure 2.1	Encourage customers to complain	7
Figure 2.2	If we get 50% of our dissatisfied customers to complain	7
Table 2.1	Differences between qualitative and quantitative research methods	9
Table 2.2	Guidelines for using quantitative research methodologies	10
Table 2.3	Four scaling properties: description and examples	12
Figure 2.3	Frequency of ratings versus rating score for each attribute	13
Table 2.4	Relationships between scale levels and measures of central tendency and dispersion	14
Table 2.5	Summary of the advantages and disadvantages of using qualitative research methods	16
Table 2.6	Relative standing or your company relative to several competitors	19
Figure 2.4	Equity diagram	21
Figure 2.5	Equity curve example	21
Figure 2.6	Getting back to the equity line	22
Figure 3.1	Customer loyalty	28
Table 3.1	Attributes of a survey design	30
Table 3.2	Organization of a typical questionnaire	31
Table 3.3	Standard deviation calculation	36
Figure 3.2	Effect of standard deviation	37
Figure 3.3	The normal distribution	39
Table 3.4	Histogram data for the two golfers	40
Figure 3.4	Histograms for the two golfers	41
Table 3.5	Single factor ANOVA summary	43
Table 3.6	Single factor ANOVA results	43
Figure 3.5	Driving distance needed for a statistically significant conclusion when the standard deviation of Golfer 2 is unchanged	44
Figure 3.6	Driving distance needed for a statistically significant conclusion when the standard deviation of Golfer 2 is made smaller	45

x List of figures and tables

Figure 4.1	Chi-squared probability density function	52
Table 4.1	Respondent's average rating	53
Table 4.2	Raw scores for responses from first time respondents	53
Table 4.3	Rank calculation for rating scores	54
Table 4.4	Sum of ranks analysis for first time respondents	54
Table 4.5	Rank calculation for rating scores	56
Table 4.6	Sum of ranks analysis for first-time non-respondents	57
Figure 5.1	Generic fishbone diagram	61
Table 5.1	Reason for poor communication	65
Figure 5.2	Number of calls affected	66
Figure 5.3	Cost of poor customer service ($)	66
Figure 5.4	The Plan, Do, Study, Act cycle	69
Table 5.2	Performance – importance analysis	74
Figure 5.5	The five types of people in any organization	78
Table 5.3	The differences between management and leadership attributes	80
Figure 6.1	Low achievable goal	85
Figure 6.2	Marginally achievable goal	85
Figure 6.3	Stretch goals	86
Figure 7.1	Final inspection only	99
Figure 7.2	Internal audit and inspection	100
Figure 8.1	Normal distribution	105
Figure 8.2	Customer requirements compared	106
Figure 8.3	Improved machine tolerance	107
Table 8.1	Decision process	108
Table 8.2	A process in control	111
Figure 8.4	Upper and lower control limits	111
Table 8.3	Sample data for the control chart example	112
Table 8.4	Abbreviated table of control chart constants	113
Figure 8.5	x-bar chart for the example problem	114
Figure 8.6	R-chart for the example problem	114
Table 8.5	Sample points from inspection data	115
Figure 8.7	x-bar chart for the samples taken on that day	115
Figure 8.8	R-chart for the samples taken on that day	116
Figure 8.9	Process with sample measurements outside of the control limits	117
Figure 8.10	Process measurements trending out of control	117
Figure 8.11	Graph of some possible outcomes in a control chart	117

Preface

As I teach and consult about quality issues, I see that customer satisfaction is a topic that gets a lot of attention. It also is a concept that is poorly understood within the total quality system. This is caused by a "feeling" we have that we instinctively know what customer satisfaction is. We are consumers; we know what satisfies us connected to the products and services encountered in our business or personal lives. This feeling is an accurate (albeit qualitative) assessment of satisfaction that will inform our future decisions about whether to purchase a product or service and whether we would recommend it to a friend or colleague.

What we don't know is the nature of, or how much effort went into, creating that "feeling" in us. What process has the provider put in place to get us to feel good about the product or service? What are the elements that combine to deliver that sense of satisfaction? This book gives insights into the process that companies can use to create that satisfaction in their customers and promote loyal behavior in customers' buying patterns. Satisfaction is a feeling; loyalty is a behavior that has satisfaction as its foundation coupled with a willingness to repurchase and a willingness to recommend. It is that interest in reliving a positive customer experience that creates loyal behavior.

Each chapter in this book is constructed as a self-contained entity. There is no appendix to reference for additional materials. The basic process needed to analyze and implement a robust quality system for improving customer satisfaction is incorporated in each chapter. A reader who wants to learn more about any particular method can easily reference the many books available on each topic.

In fact, the rationale for this book is to document the integrated approach I take in analyzing customer satisfaction and making recommendations to a company's management team. It is written to define the strategy and tactics needed to improve satisfaction in ways that are most important to your customers. The integrated method will help you collect data from your customers, understand the information through analysis of the metrics and comments, find root causes of problems, motivate people to contribute to improving satisfaction, and then sustain the gains by audit. I believe you will find the calculation of customer satisfaction metrics to be of particular interest in presenting the data of "customer satisfaction values" in a way that makes it easy to understand.

Some may find the math in this book to be outside their interests. The math is included to accommodate those who are interested in being practitioners and those who are not turned off by the details. Don't dismay if you don't like math. Simply take from this book the ideas that help you understand and implement an improved customer satisfaction process and leave the analysis to other members of your team who can contribute their quantitative skills to the effort. You might even gain some quantitative understanding along the way.

Sheldon D. Goldstein, P.E.
Carmel, IN
2009

1
Introduction

"Quality is never an accident; it is always the result of high intention, sincere effort, intelligent direction and skillful execution; it represents the wise choice of many alternatives."

William A. Foster

Many customer satisfaction programs start and end by soliciting customers for their satisfaction opinions and then making a pledge to improve satisfaction next year. What's wrong with that? For starters, we must look at the methods used to collect customer satisfaction data. Were the satisfaction measures collected with an unbiased survey? Were all customers surveyed or only some? If only some customers were surveyed, how does that represent the entire population of customers? What questions were asked? How were those questions compiled? How was the data evaluated? What specifically will be done to add value to our customer delivery system? Do we have the resources and commitment to deliver the improvements our customers require?

Accumulating feedback does not necessarily mean constructing unbiased survey instruments that are intended to probe the many "touch points" the company has with the customer. Many surveys query customer satisfaction with attributes *the company* believes are important. These same companies neglect to ask customers which attributes are important to *them*. This means we may be surveying the wrong attributes and improving products and services that have little or no importance to our customers. A pledge to do better is far from a plan to do better, which would include known costs, payback, objectives, deadlines, and responsibilities.

This book demonstrates the process of discovering the attributes that are important to your customers, measuring customer satisfaction with an unbiased survey instrument, analyzing that data, doing a statistical analysis to determine the best approach to improving the low-rated attribute(s), and implementing change that has a higher probability of improving customer satisfaction in the long run.

Along the way we will visit topics such as the equity curve and benchmarking to give us a better understanding of our mission and how the industry views our performance in comparison to a standard made up of the other suppliers we consider to be our competitors. This book is not a complete treatise on any one topic; rather, it is a process you can follow to improve your business in a structured way that has a good likelihood of improving customer satisfaction if implemented properly.

Big Picture versus Details

Continuous improvement is the goal of any forward-thinking organization. Whether the goal is continuously reducing cost in its various manifestations, optimizing productivity, expanding the customer base, or growing product lines, we always want to improve. We think about customer satisfaction in the same way, but the relationship we have with our customers is complicated. If we consider all the attributes that contribute to the value proposition we deliver to our customers (such as product, service, price, delivery, inventory, specifications, warranty, and design support), we can see that there are many ways customers count on us to perform. Each of these attributes has a differing level of importance to each customer. While we spend time assessing aggregate metrics for all our customers, we must also be aware that not all customers look at our performance through the same lens. Some customers weigh our performance on price very highly. Others feel that a competitive price is all that is needed; they are willing to pay for a strong warranty policy that protects them from future liability.

One important benefit of a detailed survey of our customers is that we get to know them as individuals and learn their special needs. Then, as we evaluate overall satisfaction numbers for customers in aggregate, we can use the details we have learned to address the individual needs of each of our customers.

Different Types of Feedback

When we study customer satisfaction, we often accumulate information in a variety of forms. We can measure satisfaction with a metric scale where "1" means extremely dissatisfied and "10" means extremely satisfied. Or, we can use a 5-point or 7-point scale with no numeric values. This scale uses narrative values such as "definitely disagree" to "definitely agree" to measure a statement such as "The company provides on-time delivery." This response scale can be used with or without intermediate descriptors. It relies on anchoring responses on the high end and the low end. The most important responses usually are the ones in the "comments" section, not those that are driving metrics. These comments give us an insight into how our customers think and provide details about how we should address their concerns or leverage on those qualities that they consider our strengths.

We will look at both types of response to get as much as we can from the numeric measurements that answer the question "Are we getting better?" and from the verbatim responses to the question "Are we concentrating on the improvement activities that mean the most to our customers?"

Transitioning From Information to Results

Once we have data from our customers, we must use that information to effect meaningful change. Let's say that we know our on-time delivery needs improvement in comparison to our other attributes. What should we do to find the underlying causes of our perceived poor delivery and then implement a solution? How will we measure the effectiveness of our solution and how will we sustain the improvement into the future? We will address in later chapters the topics of root cause analysis, project plans to implement changes in procedures, and measurements to confirm that improvements are durable.

2
Ask Your Customers What They Want

> *"Quality in a product or service is not what the supplier puts in. It is what the customer gets out and is willing to pay for. A product is not quality because it is hard to make and costs a lot of money, as manufacturers typically believe. This is incompetence. Customers pay only for what is of use to them and gives them value. Nothing else constitutes quality."*
>
> Peter F. Drucker

We deceive ourselves by thinking that we understand what our customers want in terms of products and services. Despite years of providing value to these customers, we really can't say we know what is important to them in our business relationship unless we make a habit of asking them directly.

The question of statistical validity always comes up. Whether a customer satisfaction study has statistical validity or not depends on the type of survey we employ and the way we achieve customer participation. For example, if we want to know how much average revenue we collected last year from each of our market segments, we can look into our database and get an average value with no uncertainty. After all, we know all our shipments and all our invoices, so the data is complete on all our customers and we know precisely how to answer that question.

Now let's ask how much revenue we can expect from each of our customers in the coming year. We can survey our customers and ask them. Some will respond and many will not respond. If we have enough responses (the details of how to calculate how many is enough will be covered in Chapter 3), we can estimate the average revenue based on the respondent's answers with a confidence level and margin of error we can calculate. What we will discover in the next chapter is that customer satisfaction is a quantity that cannot be presented in a way that uses formal statistical terminology. By this we mean that it is not the case that we can say "I am 95% certain that our level of customer satisfaction on warranty service is 86% +/− 2.3%." However, if we want our satisfaction metrics to exceed 90% in each attribute category, we don't need a sophisticated statistical analysis to conclude that we should be addressing warranty service because it is lower, on average, than our goal.

What is the benefit of asking customers what they want and how they feel about the products and services we provide? After all, if we ask them these open-ended questions, aren't we leaving ourselves open to bad news? Aren't we admitting that our working relationship might be less than satisfactory? If we believe that we might get less than a sparkling answer, why didn't we do something about it long ago?

Good questions! The reason we ask our customers to give us both the good news and the bad is because most customers, if left to their own decisions, would never tell us that something is wrong. I know that this concept flies in the face of experience. Most of us get those customer complaints in numbers far greater than customer appreciation calls. In fact, when we get a call in appreciation for something we did right, we thank the caller profusely. There may be (or at least it seems) only one congratulatory call to every 100 complaints. But the research belies that. Why do most customers fail to complain? Customers don't complain because it is usually much easier for them to take their business elsewhere. They can simply go to a competitor rather than waste time giving us negative information. By approaching them, we attempt to discover information we would not get otherwise.

In fact, when a customer has a complaint and we satisfy it quickly, we can generate greater satisfaction and loyalty with that customer than with the customer who never had a complaint. Again, that seems counterintuitive. However, the argument is as follows. A customer who complains and is satisfied quickly has experienced another service of our company. When it comes time to purchase again, that customer will have confidence knowing that a problem will be resolved quickly and to their satisfaction, a confidence they do not have with your competitor.

It would be bad planning to use this as a strategy to improve customer satisfaction, but it is strong motivation to consider superior customer service as a priority for investment. The decision trees in Figures 2.1 and 2.2 show the result of getting customers to complain and then doing something about it.

In Figure 2.1, only 20% of customers complain. As result, we retain 48% of our customers. Note that of those dissatisfied customers who do not complain, we still retain 39%. They may be held hostage to your organization, or they may be willing to give you another try.

In Figure 2.2, we have asked customers for their input and encouraged them to complain. Having increased the number of complainers from 20% to 50%, we have increased retention from 48% (48 of the original 100 dissatisfied customers) to 63%!

Ask Your Customers What They Want 7

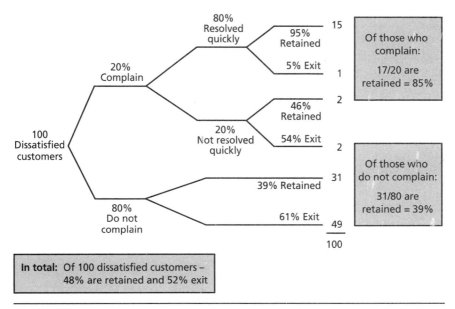

Figure 2.1 Encourage customers to complain.

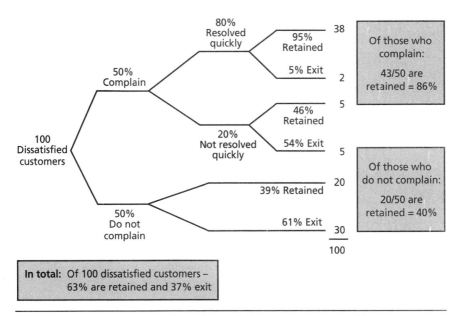

Figure 2.2 If we get 50% of our dissatisfied customers to complain.

As these decision trees demonstrate, getting customers to complain can result in maintaining more of your customers. We all know it is less expensive to keep existing customers than it is to find new ones.

GATHERING DATA AND USING RATING SCALES

> *"Quality questions create a quality life. Successful people ask better questions, and as a result, they get better answers."*
>
> Anthony Robbins

Gathering Data

How should we accumulate data about our customers? There are many ways companies poll customers—mail questionnaires, phone surveys, store intercept methods, focus groups, e-mail questionnaires, and mail panels, to name a few. The approach we will review in this book is the phone survey. We center our attention on this method because the phone survey can include both metric responses (quantitative data) and verbatim responses to open-ended questions (qualitative data).

Table 2.1 highlights the differences between qualitative and quantitative methods for accumulating data. Both are important.

Quantitative Data

Quantitative data are useful because they allow us to establish baselines for performance and compare performance year to year. A numeric response can be averaged for many respondents and for many attributes of performance.

Quantitative data include customer responses to questions such as this: "On a scale of 1 to 10, where a rating of 1 means 'very dissatisfied' and a rating of 10 means 'very satisfied,' how would you rate (company) on this statement? 'The warranty period suits my business needs.'" Using the responses from all customers, you could then aggregate the data to calculate a *mean*, an average that describes the consolidated views of all customers to that question. In that way, a rating of 8.3 in year 200x could be compared to the rating of that same attribute in the next year to assess customers' perceptions that the level of performance has slipped or improved.

Indicators direct us in the use of quantitative methods as opposed to qualitative response surveys. Table 2.2 shows some uses for quantitative studies.

Table 2.1 Differences between qualitative and quantitative research methods.[1]

Factors/characteristics	Qualitative methods	Quantitative methods
Research goals/objectives	Discovery and identification of new ideas, thoughts, feelings, preliminary insights on and understanding of ideas and objects	Validation of facts, estimates, relationships, predictions
Type of research	Normally exploratory designs	Descriptive and causal designs
Type of questions	Open-ended, semi-structured, unstructured, deep probing	Mostly structured
Time of execution	Relatively short time frames	Usually significant longer time frames
Representatives	Small samples, limited to the sampled respondents	Large samples, normally good representation of target populations
Type of analyses	Debriefing, subjective, content, interpretive, semiotic analyses	Statistical, descriptive, causal predictions and relationships
Researcher skills	Interpersonal communications. Observations, interpretive skills	Scientific, statistical procedure, and translation skills; and some subjective interpretive skills
Generalizability of results	Very limited; only preliminary insights and understanding	Usually very good; inferences about facts, estimates of relationships

Table 2.2 Guidelines for using quantitative research methodologies.[2]

Quantitative research methods are appropriate when decision makers or researchers are:

- Validating or answering a business problem or opportunity situation or information requirements.
- Obtaining detailed descriptions or conclusive insights into the motivation, emotional, attitudinal, and personality factors that influence marketplace behaviors.
- Testing theories and models to explain marketplace behaviors or relationships between two or more marketing constructs.
- Testing and assessing the reliability and validity of scale measurements for investigating specific market factors, consumer qualities (for example, attitudes, emotional feelings, preferences, beliefs, perceptions), and behavioral outcomes.
- Assessing the effectiveness of their marketing strategies on actual marketplace behaviors.
- Interested in new-product/service development or repositioning current products or service images.
- Segmenting and/or comparing large or small differences in markets, new products, services, or evaluation and repositioning of current products or service images.

Once we know that quantitative results are required, we must choose a scale for accumulating that data.

Types of Quantitative Data

There are four types of quantitative data scales. They are:

1. Nominal
2. Ordinal
3. Interval
4. Ratio

The simplest scale is the *nominal scale*. It is used for categorization such as hot or cold, like or dislike. It conveys a status, but no further information can be gleaned from this data. Nominal data can be used in analysis by proportions; for instance, 76% of respondents reported using the product.

The next scale is the *ordinal scale*, which gives us more information about the data. An ordinal scale such as good/better/best allows us to categorize data; it also gives us information about the order of preference or "acceptability" of attributes. Universities use this scale to categorize students into freshmen, sophomores, juniors, or seniors.

In an *interval scale*, differences between ratings are meaningful. We use numbers to substitute for the ordinal scale descriptions. For example, on a temperature scale the difference between 70 degrees Fahrenheit and 90 degrees Fahrenheit is 20 degrees; this has the same definition as the 20-degree difference between 120 degrees and 140 degrees. Differences are meaningful, but the value of zero degrees does not mean a total absence of temperature.

Ask Your Customers What They Want **11**

The *ratio scale* incorporates all of the attributes of the nominal, ordinal, and interval scales and adds the feature of an absolute zero. In this way, ratio-scaled data can be analyzed using the most sophisticated statistical methods. An example of a ratio scale question would be:

"How often in the last month did you call the help desk?"
_____ # of times

You can see that six times is twice three times and the intervals are also meaningful. Calling the help desk eight times as opposed to six times is the same increase as calling it four times as opposed to two times. It's not the same percentage increase, but it is the same numerical increase. We can use other mathematical techniques to analyze percentage data.

These scales have scaling *properties*:

- Nominal scale – Assignment
- Ordinal scale – Order
- Interval scale – Distance
- Ratio scale – Origin

The next table shows the descriptions for each of these properties. Note that we can use different scales to ask very similar questions. How we establish the scales will determine the analytical methods we must use to evaluate the results of our survey.

Choosing Scales

The information we need will determine which scale we choose. If we want to know how many times our customers call the warranty line, we would not ask: "When you have a problem, do you call the warranty line?" Instead, we would ask: "In the first six months after you purchased your (product), how many times did you call the warranty line?" The information requirement dictates the question and the scale, shown in Table 2.3.

How many options will you offer the customer to focus their response? Let's say you are interested in a continuum of answers from "Definitely Disagree" to "Definitely Agree." Here are several possible scale choices.

Forced Ranking Scale

Definitely Disagree	Generally Disagree	Slightly Disagree	Slightly Agree	Generally Agree	Definitely Agree
☐	☐	☐	☐	☐	☐

Neutral Scale

Definitely Disagree	Generally Disagree	Slightly Disagree	Neither Agree nor Disagree	Slightly Agree	Generally Agree	Definitely Agree
☐	☐	☐	☐	☐	☐	☐

Ordinal Scale

Definitely Disagree									Definitely Agree
1	2	3	4	5	6	7	8	9	10

Table 2.3 Four scaling properties: description and examples.

Scaling properties	Description and examples
Assignment property	The employment of unique descriptors to identify an object in a set. **Examples:** The use of numbers (10, 38, 44, 18, 23, and so on); the use of colors (red, blue, green, pink, and so on); yes and no responses to questions that identify objects into mutually exclusive groups.
Order property	Establishes "relative magnitudes" between the descriptors, creating hierarchical rank-order relationships among objects. **Examples:** 1st place is better than a 4th-place finish; a 5-foot person is shorter than a 7-foot person; a regular customer purchases more often than a rare customer.
Distance property	Allows the researcher and respondent to identify, understand, and accurately express absolute (or assumed) differences between objects. **Examples:** Family A with six children living at home, compared to Family B with three children at home, has three more children than Family B; differences in income ranges or age categories.
Origin property	A unique scale descriptor that is designated as being a "true natural zero" or "true state of nothing." **Examples:** Asking a respondent his or her weight or current age; the number of times one shops at a supermarket; or the market share of a specific brand of hand soap.

These scales differ. In the first scale, we have an even number of potential responses. This is called a forced scale because we require the respondent to take a stand. At the least, they must choose between slightly agreeing and slightly disagreeing. There is no middle ground.

In the second scale, we permit the respondents to choose an answer that is neutral; they neither agree nor disagree. This 7-point scale allows an "opt out" for those with no preferences or those who don't want to justify their stance. In many cases, this answer indicates that respondents have insufficient knowledge of the product or service; they use the middle response because they have no opinion, not because their opinion is neutral. It is better to have a "Not Applicable" or "Do Not Know" response for each question so those with no knowledge do not skew the data with a forced neutral response.

The third scale is anchored at both ends with a description, and it permits a more fluid interpretation on the part of the respondent. The most common numeric divisions are 1 through 5, 1 through 7, or 1 through 10. As you can see, we start with the business problem we want to solve, design a research question called a *construct* that can give us an insight into the cause of the problem, and then choose a scale to measure respondents' answers to the question. Now, what kind of data are we dealing with?

Customer Satisfaction Data

The quantitative data we collect from customer satisfaction surveys is usually a response by the customer to a question about an attribute that the company provides to its customers. A typical question would be: "Please rate on a scale of 1 to 10 (where a rating of 1 means 'Very Dissatisfied' and a rating of 10 means 'Very Satisfied'), your response to the following question: 'How satisfied are you with our punctuality?'" Of course, this question would be embedded in several questions so that the directions can be given once for all questions that use these scaling criteria.

Looking at the responses and this scale, we can see that a customer satisfaction scale is an ordinal scale. A rating of 8 is not twice the satisfaction of a rating of 4, and improving satisfaction from 5 to 6 requires a different level of effort than increasing satisfaction from 8 to 9. Since this scale does not have meaningful intervals, nor does it have a ratio property, it is ordinal. In addition, responses to this scale tend to be skewed to the left, with more people responding on the higher end of the scale than on the lower end. In fact, a typical customer satisfaction histogram looks like Figure 2.3.

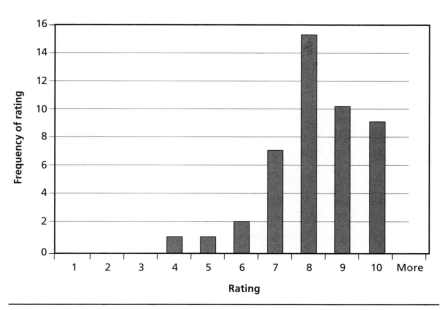

Figure 2.3 Frequency of ratings versus rating score for each attribute.

This fact limits the methods that can be used to analyze customer satisfaction data. This will be covered in depth in Chapters 3 and 4. At this point, it's obvious that we must use methods that are appropriate for ordinal data that do not rely on the assumption that data will fall into a normal distribution.

Table 2.4 illustrates the relationship between scales and the most appropriate measures of central tendency and variation that may be used to summarize the data results and what the data are telling us.

Those of us who are accustomed to using the mean and standard deviation to understand data can see that those are inappropriate measures for ordinal data sets. Rather, median and range are more appropriate to draw statistical conclusions from customer satisfaction surveys.

Table 2.4 Relationships between scale levels and measures of central tendency and dispersion.

Measurements central tendency	Five basic levels of scales				
	Nominal	Ordinal	True class interval	Hybrid ordinally-interval	Ratio
Mode	Appropriate	Appropriate	Appropriate	Appropriate	Appropriate
Median	Inappropriate	More appropriate	Appropriate	Appropriate	Appropriate
Mean	Inappropriate	Inappropriate	Most appropriate	Most appropriate	Most appropriate
Dispersion					
Frequency distribution	Appropriate	Appropriate	Appropriate	Appropriate	Appropriate
Range	Inappropriate	More appropriate	Appropriate	Appropriate	Appropriate
Estimated standard deviation	Inappropriate	Inappropriate	Most appropriate	Most appropriate	Most appropriate

Qualitative Data

There is a certain level of comfort in being able to summarize data in a numerical form. However, we miss out on rich material when we fail to ask qualitative questions in our customer surveys. This does not mean simply having a section for write-in comments. It means to seek out answers to questions such as these that can only be answered by comments: "Whom do you contact when you have a problem that must be solved immediately?" or "What could (company) do to increase your level of satisfaction?"

These questions can't be answered with a scale of 1 to 10. These questions are derived from a detailed understanding of your customers' needs. We usually gain this knowledge from talking to our customers. There are many avenues to gain this information, including:

- Sales force feedback
- Warranty claims
- Customer complaints
- Marketing surveys
- Customer purchasing preferences
- Focus groups

This information is useful in that it gives us the ability to understand the underlying reasons for customer needs. If we show that a metric scored low, we know what to work on. If we ask that question about punctuality and it scores low, say an aggregate rating of 5.3 out of 10, we know that this is a problem. But what causes the punctuality problem? The richness of responses to a follow-up question such as "How would you describe the punctuality of our employees?" will give us many and varied responses. We might expect that a respondent would say, "I waited for an hour after the promised time and he didn't show up. I had to leave work early to make the appointment and I'm angry that he was late. It would have been better if you had called me within 30 minutes of his planned arrival. I could have been home on time to let him in and not missed work!" You can't get that kind of information from a ten-point scale.

Used exclusively, neither qualitative nor quantitative data are enough. It is recommended that every customer satisfaction survey use a combination of questions specifically designed to accumulate information that is actionable and ready to be implemented to improve customer satisfaction. There are many advantages of qualitative data and also some disadvantages. Table 2.5 shows a summary of these.

Table 2.5 Summary of the advantages and disadvantages of using qualitative research methods.[3]

Advantages of qualitative methods	Disadvantages of qualitative methods
• Economical and timely data collection • Richness of the data • Accuracy of recording marketplace behaviors • Preliminary insights into building models and scale measurements	• Lack of generalizability • Inability to distinguish small differences • Lack of reliability and validity • Difficulty finding well-trained investigators, interviewers, and observers

THE IMPORTANCE OF EACH CUSTOMER-IDENTIFIED ATTRIBUTE

"In a true 'zero-defects' approach, there are no unimportant items."

Philip Crosby

The Importance of Attributes

Why work on a weakness if that attribute isn't important to your customers? There is a reason, but your satisfaction measures must be very high for you to qualify. In fact, attributes are not worth improving if there is no benefit accruing to you once they are improved.

One way to measure the importance of an attribute is to ask your customers how important it is to them. You might be surprised that some customers identify attributes not important at all when you consider them very important. In a survey that my company conducted with customers who used our commercial boilers, we asked whether same-day service was important to them. To set the stage for this question, we provided service on a 24-hour basis, sending out technicians at night if a customer called in an outage. We believed that customers demanded this service even in the dead of night. As a confirmation of this belief, we asked our customers via a mail survey what the top-three attributes were from a list of about twelve, where 24-hour service was included as one of the attributes. We also asked what the three lowest-rated attributes were from the same list. We found 24-hour service on the top-three list. It was also on the bottom-three list.

This was puzzling at first. But then we realized that customers can be segmented into those who found 24-hour service to be critically important to their businesses and another large segment that found 24-hour service to be unimportant. When we discussed this in more depth with our customers, we learned that those who needed the extra service were driven by a regulatory need to have the use of the boiler. In many other cases, customers were inconvenienced when they had to open the facility in the middle of the night and when the noise of repair annoyed those in close proximity to the boiler.

We began asking customers who called in late in the day or at night whether we could send a technician to their facility first thing in the morning. Many customers found that solution preferable, and those who absolutely needed service were accommodated. We saved a lot of overtime and customers had the choice of the best service for their business. This was a win-win solution.

Important, But to Whom?

Once we have an understanding of the importance of attributes to our customers, we must be certain that our perception matches theirs. In general, we come up with a list of attributes we believe are important to our customers and then ask them to rate their relative importance. Although that will give us a way to discriminate between attributes' importance, it doesn't guarantee that we have an exhaustive list. We must ask our customers to suggest any other attributes they believe represent value to them that may not be on the list.

Rating Importance

Once we have this complete list of attributes that our customers have confirmed are important to them, we want to put them in order from most important to least important. Again, we poll customers and ask them to rate the importance of each attribute.

On one survey we conducted, we gave all twelve attributes to our customers and asked them to rate them on a scale of 1 to 10, where a rating of 1 meant that the particular attribute wasn't important at all to them and a rating of 10 meant that the attribute was critically important. Generally, this question results in ratings of 9 or 10 for every attribute. We draw two conclusions from this result. First, customers rarely take a service or product attribute and assign it a low importance rating. No one wants to give up something they enjoy now, even if it isn't very important to them. They fear that if they rate an attribute a 3 or 4, it will be taken away because it has low importance to customers. They will have given up a benefit and received nothing for it in return. What if they need it in the future and it is no longer a part of the value package?

Another way to look at this data is to recognize that we wouldn't have included an unimportant attribute in the list, so we can expect all attributes to have high importance to our customers. In fact, by showing keen interest in all our attributes, they confirm that we have chosen excellent attributes to poll. With that information, we can accept that small differences in importance ratings probably have more discriminatory power than those same differences in other polls. Put another way, if there is a difference in *satisfaction* ratings from 9.3 to 9.4, it would be not as important as a difference in *importance* rating of 9.3 to 9.4. That is because satisfaction ratings likely have a range of responses from 5 to 10, whereas importance ratings probably have a range of responses from 8 to 10. Same means, but different variations.

If you want to find out which attributes have more importance, you can use the "top three" and "bottom three" method described in the experience that led off this section.

BENCHMARKING

"Quality has to be caused, not controlled."

Philip Crosby

Who Are Your Competitors?

Are you a local business, a national business, or an international business? Using the right benchmarks can mean the difference between real improvement and fooling yourself. As our world becomes more global in sourcing and outsourcing, many businesses must take a broader view of the competition. It is obvious that automobile manufacturers must benchmark against the world-class performers in each of their segments, but is it equally true that a local plumbing company can be satisfied comparing itself to other local plumbing companies?

The answer is complicated by the fact that a national chain could enter the market and outperform the locals at a moment's notice. Setting goals that use the right benchmarks can eliminate the surprise of a sudden entry into your market. What happens to local shops when a Wal-Mart opens up in its territory? They can compete (and usually lose), or they can distinguish themselves in a niche market and simply provide better products and services than the big-box competitors. Having the right benchmark gives you time to plan a successful strategy and provide a definition of the goal to achieve. If you don't have that goal in specific terms, you become complacent and susceptible to surprises.

How Do They Perform?

Benchmarking is much more than informal comparative analysis against a competitor. In one case of cooperative benchmarking, companies agree to share information with other organizations in their benchmarking group for the benefit of all members in the group. In "best in class" benchmarking, a company would select a company that is known to be a high performer in a selected attribute and then work on emulating this level of performance as a goal.

Generally, then, benchmarking involves some specific steps:

- Identify those attributes you want to improve.
- Identify other companies in your industry that perform at a high level in those attributes.
- Identify other industries that have similar processes and companies in those other industries that perform at high levels in those attributes.
- Establish new goals patterned after the "best practices" and performance metrics you've documented for those high-performing companies. Each attribute you want to improve may require you to choose a different company as the "best-performing" model for that particular attribute.

Merging Importance and Performance

One effective way to combine ratings and importance is to prepare a table similar to the one illustrated in Table 2.6. The critical point is to be certain that you use credible, high-performing competitors in the comparison and that the estimates for performance are predicted by persons well informed about the answers. It is tempting to rely on the opinions of your internal "experts" to fill in this form. That would be easy, but less than comforting. It is much better to ask your customers how they would rate the importance of each performance attribute and how they would rate your performance and the performance of your competitors.

Table 2.6 Relative standing of your company relative to several competitors.

Attribute	Importance (I)	Your company		Competitor 1		Competitor 2	
		Rating (R)	R x I	Rating (R)	R x I	Rating (R)	R x I
Quality	10	8	80	7	70	8	80
Delivery	8	6	48	10	80	8	64
Meeting specs	10	10	100	6	60	9	90
Price	7	7	49	8	56	5	35
Warranty	4	9	36	6	24	5	20
Total			313		290		289

Interpreting the results of your table shows where your company stands in relation to your competitors; it also shows the areas that need improvement most, and especially where improvement is needed in attributes that hold high importance with your customers. In this example, it is clear that your company is the leader with a higher R x I score than your competitors. In the area of delivery, which has a high level of importance with your customers, Competitor 1 has the lead. You have a commanding lead for warranty, but because this is an attribute that holds relatively little importance with your customer, it adds little to your overall satisfaction rating.

In other words, to get the most "bang for the buck" you must concentrate on improving those attributes that are rated lowest by your customers but prioritized highest in importance in their eyes.

CREATING THE EQUITY CURVE

"If you don't know where you are going, you might wind up somewhere else."

Yogi Berra

What kind of a business do we want to be? Not what industry or niche, but where do we stand on the price versus value diagram? Let's look at an equity diagram, shown in Figure 2.4.

On the y-axis (the ordinate scale) we have measures of value. *Value* is the delivery proposition we offer to our customers with features such as quality, delivery, cost, warranty, design support, and all those tangible and intangible features that our customers appreciate in our joint working relationship. On the x-axis (the abscissa scale) we have price. This four-quadrant box goes from the origin to the right with increasing price and from bottom to top with increasing value. The line from the lower left going to the upper right quadrant is the equity line, where the price paid for your goods and services equals the value received. We always want our business to be perceived as providing value that is justified by the price.

Which Quadrant Should We Strive to Be In?

Your company can be in any quadrant as long as you are on, or close to, the equity line. If your products or services are in the lower left quadrant (quadrant 1), you have lower quality products sold at low cost. If your products are in the upper right quadrant (quadrant 3), you have higher quality products at higher cost. Neither is better than the other. Many companies flourish selling plain-vanilla products at low cost and high volume, such as golf balls priced under $15 a dozen. Some companies function in another niche, selling high-end products such as golf balls priced over $45 a dozen. We must decide where on the value curve we want to be.

Or must we decide? Some companies want to satisfy many different market segments. In so doing, they clearly distinguish between offerings of their products to attract different groups of customers. Think in terms of Green, Gold, or Platinum American Express Cards. Figure 2.5 shows how this product family fits in the value box and covers a wide range of customer segments while being true to each brand as a distinct value story. Each of these products must be evaluated in terms of its ability to reach the equity line and provide justified value for the price.

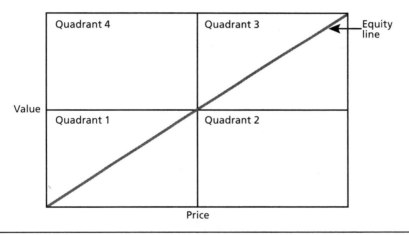

Figure 2.4   Equity diagram.

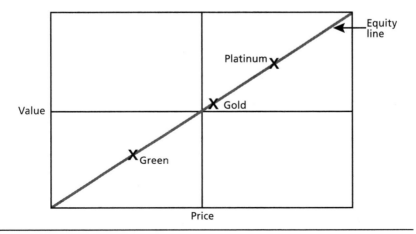

Figure 2.5   Equity curve example.

22 Chapter Two

A company in the upper left or lower right quadrants (quadrants 2 or 4), can be far away from the equity line. These quadrants are not a good place to be unless we are fairly close to the equity line.

Getting Back to the Equity Line

If we are off the equity line, our goal is to return to the line. The reason for wanting to be on the equity line is simple. Any time we are above the equity line we have provided value that the customer is not paying for, compared to our market competitors. Whenever we are below the equity line, we are charging our customers more than we provide in value. Neither of these conditions is sustainable in the long term. Leaving money on the table drains the company of vital financial resources to develop new and improved products, investors of acceptable returns, and cash to fund business expansion. Charging customers more than the market value for equivalent products and services is soon detected by customers and business is lost to our competitors. This is strong motivation to bring our business to the equity line.

Figure 2.6 shows the various ways we can get back to the equity line. If we are above the line, we can increase price at constant value (a) or decrease value at the same price (b). If we are below the line, we can decrease price at constant value (c) or increase value at the same price (d). Or, we can do a combination of the two and get back to the equity line more quickly. These different strategies result in different time periods to return to the equity line and also in different target locations on the equity line. Where do you want your business to end up?

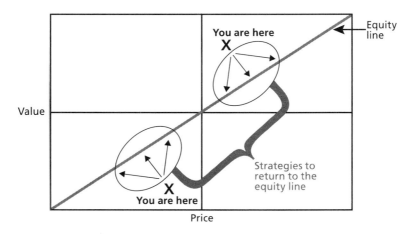

Figure 2.6 Getting back to the equity line.

Notes

1. Adapted from *Marketing Research: Within a Changing Information Environment,* Joseph F. Hair Jr., Robert P. Bush, David J. Ortinau, 3rd Ed, 2006, McGraw Hill.
2. Adapted from *Marketing Research: Within a Changing Information Environment,* Joseph F. Hair Jr., Robert P. Bush, David J. Ortinau, 3rd Ed, 2006, McGraw Hill.
3. *Marketing Research: Within a Changing Information Environment,* Joseph F. Hair Jr., Robert P. Bush, David J. Ortinau, 3rd Ed, 2006, McGraw Hill.

3
Customer Feedback and Satisfaction Metrics

"Profit in business comes from repeat customers, customers that boast about your product or service, and that bring friends with them."

W. Edwards Deming

Random Sampling

If we could survey all of our customers, there would be no reason to sample. If we knew the opinions of all our customers, there would be no uncertainty in our minds about their motivations, satisfactions, or frustrations and we could construct a roadmap of our next steps to improve customer satisfaction. However, it is usually impractical to gain the agreement of all our customers to participate in a survey, and that introduces uncertainty about whether we fully understand the nature, complexity, or completeness of customers' needs. Given our inability to survey all customers, the next best prospect is to sample them. In other words, we approach our customers and ask them to participate in the survey.

The gold standard of surveying is to have a random sample of customers. This is a cross section of all customers who have exactly the same characteristics as your total customer base, but is a smaller group than your entire customer list. For example, if we had a completely random sample of our customers, the sample would contain exactly the same percentage of customers as the population in terms of revenue, profit margin, product or service purchases, geographical location, and so on. It would look exactly like the customer population, but it would be smaller. It should be obvious that no sample will be a smaller but exact replica of our customer population. That introduces uncertainty into the results we draw from a sample. Although we can generalize from our sample to the population of our customers, we could be wrong because of the errors inherent in sampling.

Think of a poll of probable voters before an election. It is impractical to poll all voters, so we poll a small sample to project what the population would do. We have all seen the results of such polls with a stated margin of error of perhaps +/−3% or +/−4%. That is the statistical error related to random sampling as opposed to polling the entire population. Therefore, when we sample we rely on the willingness of our customers to participate in the survey. And since we can't get a response from someone who is not willing to participate, we have a sample that can be different from a fully random sample, which can introduce bias into our conclusions. When we sample, the mere act of sampling results in probable error; we can't be sure that respondents are distributed in their opinions exactly like the underlying population.

Primary versus Secondary Data

Customer satisfaction surveys fall under the strategies and tactics of marketing research. Within the context of marketing research there are two main branches: primary research and secondary research. Secondary research is the mode of inquiry that relies on existing data from which we draw conclusions. We can look into our database and determine average revenue by customer segment, warranty cost by product, or any data that we have accumulated. None of this requires the participation of our customers; we can analyze population data, completely random samples, or any subset of information we choose.

Primary data differ from secondary data because primary data are not in our database. It is a data set that we must generate from the field, and it represents a new information construct that we have never collected before. It represents an investment in time and money, usually above that required for a secondary research study, and it relies on the willingness of our customers to participate and supply us with the data we need. Some do, and some don't. That results in non-random sampling and the inherent uncertainty that results from sample surveying.

Initial Respondents

Whenever we poll customers and either send them unsolicited surveys or ask them whether they would be willing to participate in a survey, those who step up and volunteer are referred to as first-time respondents, or initial respondents. Usually, these first-time respondents have something very good to say or very bad to say. That is why they agree to participate in the survey right away. In many cases, there are more positive responses than negative responses, so the satisfaction scores tend to be skewed to the higher levels of satisfaction than the entire population. Because of this tendency of initial respondents to skew the data toward higher levels of satisfaction, it is important to make a special effort to survey those who are "merely satisfied," the initial non-respondents who declined to participate in the survey the first time.

Initial Non-Respondents

Enticing customers to participate in customer satisfaction surveys can be frustrating. In the consumer and some commercial markets, marketing research firms put a crisp, new dollar bill into the envelope with the survey. This is an attempt to bring guilt and ethical conduct into your decision about whether to participate in the survey. Most of us, upon receiving such a survey and the dollar bill, will feel guilty if we pocket the dollar and throw away the survey. It somehow offends our sense of ethical conduct. Although we would rather not spend the time to fill out the survey and the dollar is scant recompense for the commitment in time and thought required, we dutifully fill in answers because we can't accept the dollar in good conscience without filling in the survey.

Why go through all this trouble? I conducted an analysis on initial respondents and initial non-respondents at a company I ran in the early 2000s. This provider of products and services to commercial clients enjoyed a high level of customer satisfaction. In fact, we measured an average satisfaction level on eleven attributes of 91%–92% consistently. We also resent surveys to our customers who didn't respond within 30 days and we accumulated their responses separately. The first time non-respondents had an average satisfaction level of 89%, confirming our assumption that there is a difference in opinions between these two categories of survey participants.

Companies will spend time and effort to motivate even a single non-respondent to fill out a survey. In an MBA marketing research class I taught a few semesters ago, a student told us a story about having received a survey with the dollar. Being an ethical graduate student, he couldn't bring himself to fill out the survey or keep the dollar. He placed the blank survey into the return envelope along with the dollar and sent it back to the research company. I congratulated him on his conduct and then he said that the story didn't end there. About two weeks later, he received another survey from the research organization and this time it contained a $5 bill! He kept the money and filled out the survey. Apparently he had a price for compliance and $1 wasn't enough.

If you want to have a more balanced view of customer satisfaction, be sure to entice more customers to participate in the survey, including those who are reluctant when first approached.

Past Customers

There are two categories of past customers. One category includes customers who would use your company again, but who have infrequent need for your products and services. You feel that you have lost them, but they are inactive rather than disgruntled. The second category includes customers who are unhappy with your company and who are actively purchasing products and services you provide from another vendor. We want to know why they no longer purchase from you. Again, we are searching out bad news in order to improve the way we do business and appeal to a broader segment of the customer base.

Existing customers are generally happy with your company. We can learn how to better satisfy their needs, but past customers have a different perspective that gives us insight into how we lose customers. This information provides more robust challenges and perhaps the ability to solve serious issues and retain a greater percentage of our existing customer base.

Satisfaction and Loyalty

It is often said that customer satisfaction is a feeling, but customer loyalty is a behavior. In fact, some customers stay with you because they have no place else to go (they are held hostage), but in most cases they have alternatives.

How do we entice customers to be loyal to us? Clearly, it requires more than satisfaction can measure. In fact, the three measures of loyalty are satisfaction, willingness to repurchase, and willingness to recommend to others. Loyalty is measured by the intersection of satisfaction and willingness to both repurchase and recommend, as illustrated by the shaded area in Figure 3.1.

Loyalty is a behavior. It incorporates action. When conducting a satisfaction survey, one should always include two questions at the end: "Would you be willing to recommend (Company) to your colleagues and industry acquaintances?" and "Would you be willing to repurchase from (Company)?" These give us an indication of customer loyalty, because customers willing to recommend your company are also indicating that they have confidence in your company to stand behind their reference. Customers willing to repurchase are showing future intentions, usually based on prior experience. In

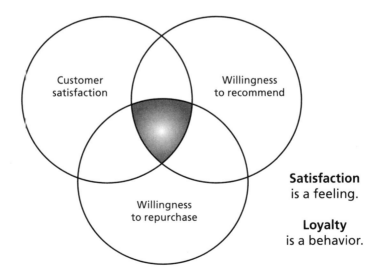

Figure 3.1 Customer loyalty.

conjunction with their response about satisfaction, it gives a strong measure of loyalty and confidence in a future relationship.

Formulating the Questionnaire

A questionnaire should be constructed to address attributes and issues that are important to your customers. As we demonstrated in Chapter 2, we need to poll our customers to ask them about those touch points that provide true value to them in their relationship with your company. This provides the framework for our survey instrument. A survey should be short enough to keep the respondent interested and long enough to accumulate all the important information needed by your company.

A model for organizing the written survey follows a simple format. First, we ask qualifying questions that are easy to answer and assure that we are talking to someone who is capable of answering the questions in a thoughtful manner. Next, we ask questions that require some interpretive skills. Then we ask focused questions that zero in on the heart of the research issues. We end with loyalty questions and an open-ended question that encourages the respondent to add any final comments. This may seem like an overly structured approach to questionnaire design, but it leads respondents into the survey and makes it easier for them to stay through until the end without reneging. The last thing we want is for a respondent to end the survey prematurely and invalidate the results we have so far.

By asking some open-ended questions, whether in a fill-in or an interview survey, we can investigate the respondent's feelings about the company and solicit information about the importance of each attribute. Importance of an attribute is considered a measure of the strength of the attribute to influence the actions of the decision maker. Those attributes that have less importance are also less motivational in terms of moving the decision maker to repurchase or recommend.

Survey design is a formulaic process, as depicted in the following tables. In this context, a research question is defined below.

Research question: The research survey should be constructed around a research question, which is different than the business question. For example, low sales in a particular product family is a business issue and a symptom of the problem. Once we discuss the probable causes of this sales shortfall, we might postulate reasons that explain the symptom. We then construct a survey to confirm that the causes we believe responsible for the shortfall in sales are confirmed by our customers. The research question may be:

> Test whether the product family for (products) is broad enough for our existing and projected customer needs.

The questionnaire may be constructed with questions that will help you analyze respondent ratings and comments to determine whether this is the underlying cause. If we're not sure what the underlying cause may be, we're only postulating that it is product breadth. In that case, the survey may include several questions. Another section of the survey may deal with acceptable distribution and another may ask about price or features.

Table 3.1 shows the attributes of a survey design, and Table 3.2 shows the organization of a typical questionnaire.

Let's look at some of the methods we could use to capture respondent opinions.

Mailed questionnaires: This is an easy approach. You simply put the questionnaire in an envelope and send it to your clients. Advantages are that you can send many questionnaires fairly inexpensively and not invest a lot of resources in capturing data. Disadvantages are that you will probably receive only about 1% to 5% return and you aren't quite sure who is answering the questionnaire. In addition, there is no opportunity to probe with follow-up questions when a fill-in response needs clarification to be useful as an improvement tool.

Web surveys: These are becoming more popular than mail surveys because of the convenient response mechanism and the low cost to reach

Table 3.1 Attributes of a survey design.[1]

Attribute	Comments
Planning what to measure What are the research questions? Decide on what is to be asked under the research issue.	Keep away from "good to know" information. Stick to "must know" information.
Formatting the questionnaire In each issue, determine the content of each question. Decide on the format of each question.	What scale will give the most information?
Question wording Determine how the question is to be worded.	Positive construct or negative.
Sequencing and layout decisions Lay out the questions in a proper sequence. Group all the questions in each subtopic to get a single questionnaire.	See the table that follows.
Pretesting and correcting problems Read through the whole questionnaire to check whether it makes sense and measures what it is supposed to measure.	Does it flow easily? Does it have buy-in from internal decision-makers? Do customers confirm the importance of the questions?

Table 3.2 Organization of a typical questionnaire.[2]

Location	Type	Function	Example
Starting questions	Broad, general questions	To break the ice and establish a rapport with the respondent	How long have you been a client?
Next few questions	Simple and direct questions	To reassure the respondent that the survey is simple and easy to answer	What products (or services) do you use?
Questions up to a third of the questionnaire	Focused questions	Relate more to the research objectives and convey to the respondent the area of research	Who is your main point of contact at our company?
Major portion of the questionnaire	Focused questions; some may be difficult and complicated	To obtain most of the information required for the research	How would you rate (company's) performance on (attribute)?
Last few questions	Closing questions	To get classification and loyalty information about the respondent	Would you recommend (company) to your colleagues?

many potential respondents. This improves response volume and response rate, but web surveys still suffer from uncertainty about who is actually responding and the lost opportunity for probing follow-up questions.

Telephone surveys: These cost much more than mail or web, and they are used in surveys that require fewer respondents. They can be employed to contact clients when it is useful to have comments to help explain a given response. For example, when a numeric scale is used to measure satisfaction with an attribute, we often want an explanation for the rating given (say 6 out of a possible 10). The company wants to know why it scored so low. It wants to learn the specifics of this relative dissatisfaction and the respondent wants to say why that score was given. A telephone interview permits the respondents to go "off-script" in hopes that the attribute will be improved if they are specific enough in explaining why they are dissatisfied.

Telephone interviews can be conducted at the convenience of the respondent. When conducting personal telephone interviews, I entice potential respondents to name a call-back time that is convenient to them, thus reducing their reluctance to participate in the survey.

Personal interview: This is perhaps the most expensive to conduct. This one-on-one approach is effective when we are looking for experts to give us information that is difficult to obtain any other way. A skilled interviewer can read body language and probe issues effectively face-to-face. It is also a good way to accumulate information on sensitive topics that would be awkward to discuss with anyone else in the room. For example, when conducting focus groups I sometimes discover that an employee is uncomfortable discussing obstacles that inhibit the provision of excellent customer satisfaction. These employees will offer to meet me privately to talk about the issue, which often involves a coworker or the supervisor. This isn't a conversation they would be able to have in a group meeting. However, when the interviewer compiles the results of the group meetings, this information can be summarized as part of the feedback to the management team. We'll talk more about this in Chapter 6.

Numerical Responses

Effective surveys employ several different processes for collecting data. I like to use numerical scales as one of the processes for several reasons. First, a numerical scale gives us a quantitative way to evaluate customer satisfaction with an attribute. We can clearly discern the difference between a rating of 7 and a rating of 9. I find a 10-point scale a natural tool. Most people think in terms of grades (a 9 out of 10 being an "A," an 8 being a "B," and so on). This scale includes more than enough gradations to be acceptable to almost all respondents. On a 5-point scale many respondents want to give a 4.5, believing it is "greater than a 4 but not as good as a 5." With a 10-point scale, that tendency is reduced.

A numeric scale has an additional advantage. If we use the same questions year after year, we can compare satisfaction ratings from year to year and see whether there is improvement. If all the responses to our survey are fill-in, it is much harder to quantify a substantive change from year to year.

Fill-in Responses

Numerical responses give us the comparative values to present customer satisfaction in an understandable way for goal setting and reporting. Verbatim responses give us the actionable items that help us improve customer satisfaction. When customers answer a question such as this ("If you could improve one thing that would increase your level of satisfaction, what would that be?"), it permits us to understand their motivations. We can then formulate action items around those responses, improving products, services, or processes that intercept customer needs precisely.

There is no way to find the answer to a qualitative question such as that by using a numeric scale. And although many questionnaires are weighted to numerical response questions, it is the qualitative responses that give us much richer information. We must be careful to note that qualitative responses cannot be generalized to the population. They are useful to understand the opinions of the respondents; if our intention is to survey influential customers, we have succeeded.

Sample Size

There are two basic ways to look at sample size. One is from the perspective of statistical significance of the data. The other is by selecting any customers who will participate in the survey. The second method doesn't sound very scientific, but in many cases it is the best we can do. We understand that we will not be able to draw statistically significant conclusions from our survey. We will survey all customers who are willing participants and stop only when we run out of customers to question or we run out of our budget. Let's look at this a bit more closely.

A satisfaction survey is primary research. It is meant to solicit information we don't have and it requires that customers agree to participate. We can't get responses from customers who refuse to participate! This introduces uncertainty into the conclusions we can draw based on the survey results. We must assume that we have a biased survey. But though it isn't as pure as we would like, there is good news: If we ask customers to participate again next year, we can expect the same kind of bias in the survey results. As long as we understand that our results are approximate, we will use the information as a guideline and not as a rigid edict. We must understand that a graph of satisfaction that shows variability with no obvious slope is probably demonstrating normal variation in the data, as in the following figure:

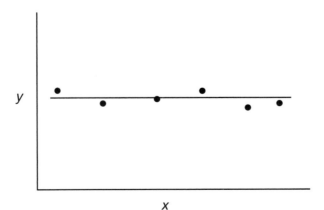

The next figure shows a graph of satisfaction scores with an obvious upward slope indicating that although there is still random variation from year to year, we can have some confidence that there is improvement over time:

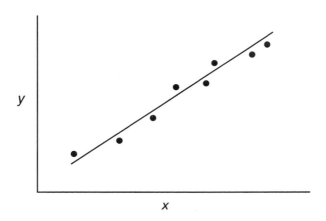

From an analysis point of view, we can tell that there is an upward trend in this data by performing a regression on the line. That topic is outside the scope of this book. Suffice it to say that interpreting satisfaction data leaves a lot to be desired in confidence, but none of us will dispute that a continuously upward trend is a very good result.

ANALYZING THE DATA (DESCRIPTIVE STATISTICS)

"It's not that I'm so smart, it's just that I stay with problems longer."

Albert Einstein

Numerical data are considered generalizable to the population and qualitative data are not. In an analysis of interval or ratio data, we can make a statement such as this: "Our research shows that there is a 95% probability that customers rate our service at a satisfaction level of 93% with a margin of error of +/−3.4%." Not so with ordinal data from customer satisfaction surveys, and not so for qualitative responses to fill-in questions. How should we analyze our satisfaction data if we can't get these statistically significant (and really comforting) results? The best way to look at ordinal data is to use the range and median of the data for our understanding of the measure of central tendency and variability of the data. The best way to look at qualitative responses is by categorization. Let's take these one by one.

ORDINAL DATA METRICS

Mean, Median, and Mode

The *mean* is the average of all the data responses. We can have a mean of any data set. The *median* is the middle value of all the data responses. It doesn't account for the actual data values; it just counts the number of responses and finds the middle value when the data are sorted from high to low or low to high. In an uneven number of responses, it is the middle value. In an even number of responses, it is the average of the two middle values.

The *mode* is the data value that occurs with the highest frequency. Many data sets have no value of mode since no observation is repeated. For instance, if we were to list the per capita income of families in each of the fifty states, there would be no mode. No two states have the same per capita income to the dollar. This measure of central tendency is useful when we are looking at categorized data and we want to see which value is reported with the highest frequency.

If we look at the following data series we can see the difference in the mean and the median:

$$1 \quad 5 \quad 10 \quad 12 \quad 22$$

The mean of this data series is the sum of the values divided by 5, or $50/5 = 10$. The median is the middle value, or 10.

Now, what if our data series looks like this:

$$1 \quad 5 \quad 10 \quad 12 \quad 502$$

The mean of this data series is $530/5 = 106$. The median of this data series is still 10.

The mean is dependent on the actual values of the data collected. The median is always the middle value; it is not affected by wide fluctuations in individual data points. An example of median is IQ scores. A score of 100 is the median score of adults in the United States. That means 50% of the people have an IQ of greater than 100 and 50% of the people have an IQ of less than 100. The median is unaffected by the actual scores and is only a measure of population percentiles. Satisfaction scores represent ordinal data sets and are best analyzed with median as the measure of central tendency, not mean. This was introduced in Chapter 2.

Range and Standard Deviation

Range and standard deviation are measures of variability of the data around the middle point. Often, when we use the median as our measure of central tendency, we use the range. When we use mean, we use standard deviation.

Range is the difference between the highest and lowest values in a data set. Although this is a crude measure of variability, it gives us an indication for the dispersion of data around the median. For example, we can have a data set that consists of observations such as these:

$$10 \quad 11 \quad 12 \quad 13 \quad 14 \quad 15 \quad 16$$

The mean and median are both 13, and the range is 16 – 10, or 6.

Another data set might be:

$$5 \quad 10 \quad 11 \quad 13 \quad 15 \quad 16 \quad 21$$

In this case, the mean and median are both 13 again, but the range is 16. The same median, but a far different range. Similarly, *standard deviation* is a measure of variability around the mean. For a sample of data, it is calculated with this equation:

$$s = \sqrt{\frac{\Sigma (x_i - \bar{x})^2}{n - 1}}$$

Where:
s = standard deviation of the sample
x_i = each data point from 1 to n
$\bar{x}$ = mean of the data set
n = number of data points
Σ = add up the values (in this case the squared difference of all the x_i values from the mean of the data set)

Table 3.3 shows us how to calculate the standard deviation.

Table 3.3 Standard deviation calculation.

	x-values	x-mean	(x-mean) squared	
	10	–3	9	
	11	–2	4	
	12	–1	1	
	13	0	0	
	14	1	1	
	15	2	4	
	16	3	9	
mean of x-values =	13		28	= sum of sq. diff.
		Std. Dev. =	2.16025	

In this case n = 7 observations (*x*-values), and the sum of the squared differences is 28; that is, $\Sigma (x_i - \bar{x})^2$. Then

$$s = \sqrt{\frac{28}{6}} = 2.16025$$

When we have a normal distribution of data, commonly called the normal curve or the bell curve, the "flatness" of the curve is indicative of increasing or decreasing dispersion of data around the mean. For example, take the following two normal distributions and compare the standard deviations in Figure 3.2.

These two distributions have the same mean, but different standard deviations. There is more dispersion around the mean with one than with the other. This has important meaning when we talk about the confidence of our calculations.

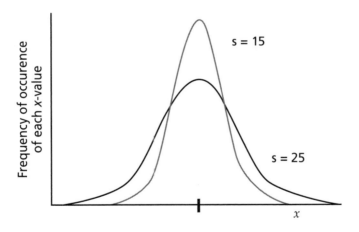

Figure 3.2 Effect of standard deviation.

As an example, look at the observations in the following two tables for observations of the driving distance of two golfers. Under the same conditions, these golfers recorded ten of their drives off the tee.

Golfer 1	Golfer 2
225	225
220	240
231	190
224	250
218	227
220	255
230	170
210	230
215	240
225	190
Mean = 222.0	222.0
Std. Dev. = 6.15	28.10

Both golfers average 222 yards off the tee, but there is a lot more variability (uncertainty) as to how far golfer 2 will hit the ball. Another way to look at this is with the range. All the observations are from 210 to 231 yards for golfer 1, but between 170 and 255 yards for golfer 2. Certainly when golfer 1 hits a drive, s(he) is fairly certain as to the distance the ball will go. Golfer 2 is uncertain about how far the ball will go, an important distinction when there is a hazard to carry. Think of a water hazard that requires a carry of 190 yards. Golfer 1 is confident because s(he) doesn't usually hit the ball any less than 210 yards. Golfer 2 may wonder whether this particular drive will carry the water, despite the fact that golfer 2 can hit the ball the same average distance as golfer 1, and in some cases much farther. It is that increased variability that raises the specter of uncertainty. To use data as a predictive tool, we want as little variability as possible.

The normal distribution has a very specific shape and known properties. The next figure shows the probability of occurrence of events defined by the normal distribution regardless of the value of the mean or standard deviation. The distribution can be flatter (having a larger standard deviation) or a narrower shape that is more indicative of a smaller standard deviation, but the area under the curve, the probability of an event, still follows the rule shown in Figure 3.3.

Using this information, we can say that 95% of golfer 1's drives will fall within +/- 2 standard deviations of the mean of 222 yards, or between 209.7 and 234.3 yards. However, since golfer 2 has a much higher standard deviation, we can be 95% sure that his (her) drives will be between 165.8 and 278.2 yards. Same rule, just calculated based on the difference in the variability of the two golfers' drives.

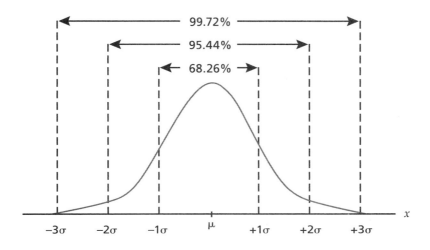

Figure 3.3 The normal distribution.

Histograms

A histogram is a tool we use to graphically show data. Histograms require us to make assumptions about the organization of data in our data set. For example, the histogram for each of the golfers is shown in Figure 3.4. The first choice we made is how to consolidate the drives into "bins" or ranges for our data. In this case, we used a 10-yard bin width for each golfer (see Table 3.4). There is no magic number for bin width. We are simply trying to show the underlying distribution of drives; if a 15-yard bin width shows this distribution better, then that is what we should use.

For those who want a place to start, you may approximate the number of bins with this equation: $2^{k-1} \geq n$; where k = # of bins
n = total number of observations

For example, if there are 50 observations in the data set, then

$k = 3$ bins: $2^{3-1} = 2^2 = 4$
$k = 4$ bins: $2^{4-1} = 2^3 = 8$
$k = 5$ bins: $2^{5-1} = 2^4 = 16$
$k = 6$ bins: $2^{6-1} = 2^5 = 32$
$k = 7$ bins: $2^{7-1} = 2^6 = 64$, this is ≥ 50, and we would start with 7 bins

The bin width is now estimated as:

$$\text{Bin width} = \frac{\text{Maximum value in the data set} - \text{Minimum value in the data set}}{7}$$

Table 3.4 Histogram data for the two golfers.

Golfer 1		Golfer 2	
Bin	Frequency	Bin	Frequency
210	1	210	3
220	4	220	0
230	4	230	3
240	1	240	2
250	0	250	1
260	0	260	1
More	0	More	0

Rounding up or down to have even numbers will help create a more "natural" grouping of data in the histogram.

Note that both distributions have the same mean, but their variability is well displayed in this format of Figure 3.4. This is a histogram and it clearly shows the more symmetric nature of the performance of golfer 1 and the heavily weighted performance of golfer 2 on lower drives.

In this format (from Microsoft Excel output), the bin has a width of 10 yards (chosen arbitrarily), and goes from 199.999 to 209.999, and so on. For golfer 1, there is only one observation in that bin, but for golfer 2, there are three observations in that bin. In fact, for golfer 2, the mean falls at a value of 221.7, but there are no observations at all in the bin 219.999 to 229.999.

In this example, there is no obvious reason to choose one bin width versus another. Our intent is to display the underlying distribution so we can understand the variation of the data. However, in many data sets there is a segmentation of data that makes sense, such as customers who spend between $10 and $50 compared to those who spend between $10,000 and $50,000. In cases where there are natural bins, or groupings of data where each group tends to act in a similar fashion, we should always consider using those natural groupings to establish our bins.

These tools help us to understand the metrics and kinds of conclusions we can draw from data that we accumulate in customer satisfaction surveys. It also gives us the background we need to recognize that no conclusion is perfect, and that there is some uncertainty in the conclusions we draw and in the recommendations we offer. Our task is to gather data in a way that minimizes uncertainty and reflects the probability that we can be wrong whenever we analyze data.

If we calculate that we are 95% sure of a conclusion we arrive at from analyzing data, it means we can be wrong 5% of the time. When we are polling voters on their favorite candidate, being right 95% of the time sounds

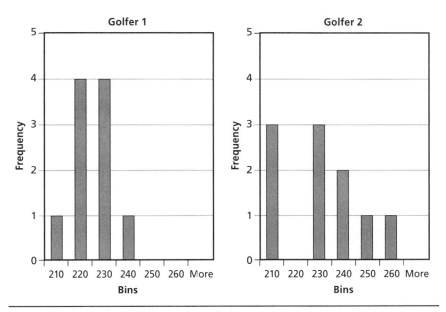

Figure 3.4 Histograms for the two golfers.

good. However, airline safety is another story. If we know that 5 of 100 flights will crash, then 95% doesn't sound good anymore. It is clear that the confidence interval we have in a conclusion depends on the application.

Qualitative Responses

These responses are the result of customers' comments. We can accumulate comments either as an explanation of a numerical response ("Let me tell you why I scored that attribute with a '6'!"), as a result of asking a fill-in question, or as a response to an open-ended question. In any case, we will have unformatted information that is almost impossible to categorize. Any attempt to fit these verbatim responses into neat groupings of information will inevitably lead us to assumptions that are unsubstantiated by the customers' comments or to an interpretation that is wrong. Unless we can segregate responses into binomial sets such as favorable or unfavorable or obviously similar responses, we must use the verbatim responses for what they are: precise comments that give us information from a specific customer. There are exceptions. For example, if we ask this question, "Would you recommend our company to your industry acquaintances?", we might get responses such as these:

- "Yes."
- "Absolutely!"
- "I have already."
- "Sure."

We would agree that these may be categorized as positive responses. Of course we might lose the magnitude of the response if we stopped there, but the idea is the same. When we get qualitative information, we should appreciate it for what it is: rich feedback that requires analysis on a case-by-case basis.

WHICH ATTRIBUTES DIFFER FROM THE OTHERS?

> *"Two roads diverged in a wood, and I—I took the one less traveled by, and that has made all the difference."*
>
> Robert Frost

Which is larger, 85 or 82? Think before you answer. It should be obvious that this is a trick question. By the time you reach the end of this chapter, you will answer, "I need more information before I can say." Why are we uncertain about a seemingly simple comparison of two numbers? Because 85 isn't always 85 and 82 isn't always 82. Let's look at an example.

When we conduct customer satisfaction surveys, we question our customers about a number of attributes. One question might be: "Please rate on a scale of 1 to 10, where 1 means you are very dissatisfied and 10 means you are very satisfied, your response to this statement: 'We arrived on time for your service.'" We expect to receive many different ratings to this question, and the average of the responses may be 8.5, or 85%. Was every response 8.5? Of course not. As shown in Chapter 2, there will be a left-skewed distribution of those responses, but the point is this. This attribute rated an average score of 85%. There is a distribution of responses that are not 85%, but we say that this is our 85% distribution. In other words, most of the responses in that distribution are indistinguishable from 85%.

Not Just Different, Statistically Different

That is a heavy concept, but it is supported by statistical theory. Let's redefine the question. First we ask again, "Is 85 larger than 82?" As a point estimate, we conclude 85 is larger than 82. For example, if one person has 85 roses and the other has 82 roses, we conclude that the person with 85 has more roses.

However, we can ask the question another way: "Are we 95% certain that the distribution with an average of 85 is larger than the distribution with an average of 82?" Then we have more work to do! Let's look at that golf example again from earlier in this chapter. Both golfers average a 222-yard drive, but with different standard deviations. Golfer 2 has more variability in distance. Not every drive is exactly 222 yards long. If we add the component of variability, we can say that there is a range over which golfer 2 can drive the ball where the individual observations (drives) are indistinguishable from the mean of 222 yards, even though they are numerically different. All drives in golfer 2's distribution are referred to as the 222-yard average drive.

In determining whether two distributions differ from each other, we use a method called analysis of variance, or ANOVA. This method analyzes both distributions in terms of their means and standard deviations to learn, with our stated demand for certainty, whether the means really are statistically different. Notice we are not asking whether the point estimates represented by the means are different, but rather whether there is a statistically significant difference in the means at the 95% confidence level. In fact, if we maintain the same standard deviations as our original example and simply increase the length of drive for golfer 2, then golfer 2 must hit the ball 242 yards on average before there is a statistically significant difference in those drives in comparison with golfer 1. Table 3.5 shows the results of this analysis. The p-value in the table is a measure of the potential for error in the analysis and is compared to 1.0 minus our confidence level. If we want to be 95% right, we are willing to be 5% wrong. The amount we expect to be wrong is the p-value. This p-value must be less than the acceptable amount we are willing to be wrong for us to claim statistical significance in our results. For a 9% confidence level, we will not accept any result that has a p-value greater than .05. If we did, we would be less than 95% confident in our result. Take a look at Tables 3.5 and 3.6.

Next, we can show what this looks like graphically. In the original example, both golfers had a mean driving distance of 222 yards. As we increase the driving distance of golfer 2, the golfer 2 distribution begins to

Table 3.5 Single factor ANOVA summary.

Groups	Count	Sum	Average	Variance
Golfer 1	10	2220	222	37.77778
Golfer 2	10	2420	242	789.3333

Table 3.6 Single factor ANOVA results.

Source of Variation	SS	df	MS	F	P-value	F crit
Between Groups	2000	1	2000	4.83611	0.041181	4.413873
Within Groups	7444	18	413.5556			
Total	9444	19				

move away from the golfer 1 distribution. The table results indicate that golfer 2 must have an average drive of 242 yards before there is a statistical difference in means. The two distributions appear to go from overlapping to very little overlapping as golfer 2's average driving distance increases. Only then can we say golfer 2's driving distance has a statistically different length at the 95% confidence level. Our conclusion is that if golfer 2 hits the ball on average 230 yards, even though 230 yards is numerically different than 222 yards, those two averages are not statistically different. Golfer 2 must hit the ball 242 yards for there to be a difference with the 222 yard driving average of golfer 1, given their respective standard deviations of their distributions. See Figure 3.5.

Now, what affects that result? It is not just driving distance but the standard deviations as well. If golfer 2 would become more consistent and lower the standard deviation of his (her) distribution, it would take less of a difference in average drives to show a statistically significant difference in their means. Visualize the distributions moving farther apart from each other as the means change. Overlap disappears sooner if the standard deviation of golfer 2 is reduced, as shown in Figure 3.6.

The same goes for comparison of attributes in a customer satisfaction survey. The more variability there is in the responses to a question, the less significant are differences in the averages. In some cases there will be a statistically significant difference between two attributes whose ratings are 85% and 82%, and in some cases there will not be a statistically significant difference between those same averages.

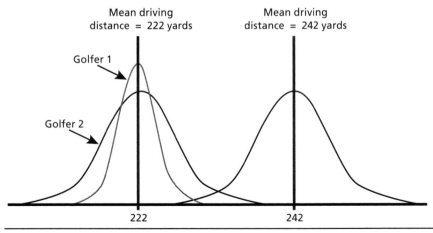

Figure 3.5 Driving distance needed for a statistically significant conclusion when the standard deviation of Golfer 2 is unchanged.

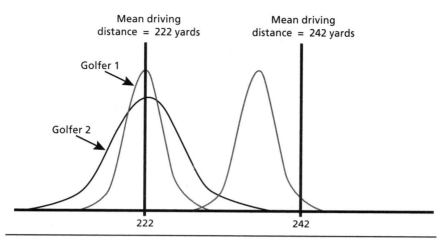

Figure 3.6 Driving distance needed for a statistically significant conclusion when the standard deviation of Golfer 2 is made smaller.

Notes

1. Adapted from *Marketing Research*, David A. Aaker, V. Kumar, George S. Day, 9th Ed, 2007, John Wiley & Sons, Inc.
2. Adapted from *Marketing Research*, David A. Aaker, V. Kumar, George S. Day, 9th Ed, 2007, John Wiley & Sons, Inc.

4
Comparing the Data (Rank Order Analysis)

*"Do not worry about your difficulties in Mathematics.
I can assure you mine are still greater."*

Albert Einstein

We learned in Chapter 2 that the use of mean and standard deviation is not appropriate for customer satisfaction data. In this case, we must find a method to draw conclusions about ordinal data. We know that every distribution has a mean; however, when we measure the mean score for two attributes and they differ, we would like to know which one represents higher satisfaction than the other, if we can. From the analysis in Chapter 3, we can use an ANOVA for interval or ratio data to calculate whether an attribute rating of, say 85% is statistically different from another attribute that is rated 82% by our customers. Why is this important? It is important because we would want to concentrate our efforts to improve customer satisfaction on those attributes that rate the lowest. If a rating of 85% and a rating of 82% are not statistically different, then working on one versus the other is arbitrary. But if they differ statistically, we can have high confidence that working on the lower ranked attribute is the appropriate way to set our priorities. With ordinal data, we want to answer an additional question. How can we determine the statistical difference between two attributes that are rated with an ordinal number system? This is where a non-parametric analysis technique can help us.

Background

There is no benefit in improving business attributes that are not likely to measurably increase customer satisfaction. The use of the *Kruskal-Wallis one-way analysis of variance by ranks* method to compare the means of satisfaction scores of several company attributes that are important to your customers can focus attention on those attributes in need of the most improvement. A statistical approach can provide confidence in identifying valid problems and recommending solutions that have a better chance of resulting in improved satisfaction.

Many customer satisfaction programs start and end with a measure of customer satisfaction and a pledge to improve. It is much harder, and perhaps less common, for company personnel to evaluate the details of customer feedback surveys, determine which company attributes may result in increases in customer satisfaction (if improved), and then set out to implement changes that are recommended by customers.

However, just because a company attribute has a low customer satisfaction measure doesn't mean it differs statistically from the other attributes important to customers. Improving the right attributes maximizes the use of resources and improves chances of a positive return on efforts.

Dimensions of the Analysis

Let's consider an example that uses data of customer satisfaction surveys to illustrate the method. Customers were surveyed to choose those attributes they thought were most important when considering service from the company. They said that the most important attributes this company could provide to meet their needs and generate high levels of satisfaction are:

- Courtesy
- Scheduling a convenient time for service
- Arriving when promised to perform the service
- Competitive pricing
- Providing overall value

Using this information, the company mailed customer satisfaction surveys each month to all customers who purchased products or services. This assured each survey corresponded to a current service and minimized the need for customers to recollect a service that occurred long ago or consolidate their feelings for several services. If we are to take control over declining customer satisfaction, we want timely feedback.

The company enjoyed a high response rate of 20% on survey returns. However, 80% of customers did not respond. Recognizing that initial non-respondents to the feedback survey tend to have different opinions about the service than first-time respondents, and therefore they display different customer satisfaction metrics, the company went to considerable effort to solicit and receive first-time non-respondent survey information to round out the information profile. Initial non-respondents were contacted again, 30 days later, with a repeat request for feedback.

These two groups were separated because they are considered to have different opinions of the company's performance in each attribute. We wanted to see whether there are indeed any differences in the conclusions we would measure from these groups.

Methodology

The premise of this analysis is that we can take a statistical approach to analyze the details of customer satisfaction surveys and determine which attributes are most favorably scored by customers and which need improvement.

We must be careful every time we draw statistical conclusions from data. In this case, there are important issues because of the nature of satisfaction data in general.

Statistical Considerations

We have compiled measures of performance for each of the five attributes. We asked respondents to rate the attributes on a scale of 1 to 10. This represents an ordinal scale. Ordinal scales do not have meaningful intervals. For example, the difference between a satisfaction improvement from 5 to 6 does not necessarily require the same level of effort as an improvement from 8 to 9. Neither is there a ratio scale. A score of 8 is not twice the level of satisfaction of a score of 4.

For these reasons, it is not strictly appropriate to use standard statistical methods to evaluate customer satisfaction metrics if the underlying probability distribution isn't normal. However, this is often done. One rationale for using statistical metrics such as mean and standard deviation for ordinal data is that we understand the limitations of interpreting the results. Another is that we usually have large sample sizes.

The non-normality of the underlying population brings discomfort to those who want to meet the requirements of an ANOVA analysis. In satisfaction data we rarely have a normal distribution. Instead, we look toward the Kruskal-Wallis test, which gives us a way to evaluate ordinal data in more depth and draw strict statistical interpretations from the results, including comparison of means.

Statistical Significance and Random Variation

We ask whether there is a difference between attribute means from a statistical perspective because we want to know whether we are seeing random variation in the means or whether one mean really is different from the others. For example, let's say that the mean of a satisfaction score is 9.05. That represents the mean of several (or many) respondents who scored the attribute. If we were to compile another set of scores at the same time and of the same population, in all likelihood a different sample of respondents would send in surveys. Some respondents would be the same and some would be different, but the sample would differ from the one summarized in this analysis. Since both samples would be measuring the same population at the same time, any difference in mean scores would be caused by random variation in sampling. We would not assume that there is a statistically significant difference in those scores.

If we can assess whether the variation between the means of the different attributes is the result of random variation or whether it is the result of a distinct difference in customer satisfaction perception between these attributes, then we can work on those attributes that show enough difference from the overall responses to warrant action. Working on attributes whose lower scores are not statistically different from the others will not result in meaningful improvement in customer satisfaction.

Independence of the Samples

While the Kruskal-Wallis test can be performed on data that is not from a normal distribution and is ordinal in nature, it requires that the samples be independent. The definition of independence requires that the scoring of one attribute would not influence the scoring of another attribute. This does not mean that there can be no correlation between attributes, only that the answers don't influence each other. For example, if we advertise heavily for a product and sales increase, we may conclude that there is a correlation; increased advertising influenced sales. These events would not be independent. However, the advertising may have been totally ineffective, and sales increased because prices were drastically reduced at the same time that the advertising campaign was launched. In this case, price and sales are correlated and these events are not independent; advertising and sales, while correlated, are really independent.

In this case, customer responses to the attributes "Were we courteous" and "Competitive pricing", for example, should not influence each other. Even the attributes that are related ("price" and "value") share so little in common that we can assume that there is independence between those two attributes as well. In several survey results I have reviewed, there have been cases where price was scored low and value was scored high.

The Kruskal-Wallis Method

The *Kruskal-Wallis one-way analysis of variance by ranks* is a method of comparing different samples to calculate whether there is a statistically significant difference between the ratings of those attributes. The method relies on the ranks of the scored values and the means of those ranks, rather than examining the means of the data.

Even though there is a difference in the averages, we must not conclude that the difference is statistically meaningful. Once we decide how sure we want to be about our conclusions (in this case we are using a .05 significance level, 95% level of confidence), we conduct the Kruskal-Wallis test to decide whether any attributes are statistically different from the others with the specified degree of significance.

First, we set up a simple hypothesis test that postulates there is no difference between the satisfaction scores of any of the attributes. The null hypothesis is H_o; the research, or alternate hypothesis, is H_a.

H_o: All attribute populations are identical
H_a: All attribute populations are not identical

We assume that there is no statistically significant difference between the means in the null hypothesis (H_o). When we employ the Kruskal-Wallis test statistic, we are testing the validity of this hypothesis. This test relies on a distribution that is approximated by a Chi-squared distribution with degrees of freedom k-1, or the number of attributes being compared minus 1. The test ranks responses based on the raw data (scale of 1 to 10 responses).

The ranking of responses is performed by setting up a rank for all n_T data points and then summing the ranks of the data in each sample. We then calculate the test statistic:

$$W = \left[\frac{12}{n_T(n_T+1)} \sum_{i=1}^{k} \frac{R_i^2}{n_i} \right] - 3(n_T+1)$$

Where: k = the number of attribute samples
n_i = the number of responses in sample i
n_T = the total number of responses in all samples
R_i = the sum of the ranks for sample i

Corrections for Tied Observations

In this case, it is necessary to consider one further factor, ties in the ranks. This is referenced in most books that cover tests of ranks. Whenever the data have repeat scores, for example a rating of 9 from many respondents, the ties must be considered in a correction factor applied to the value of W to account for the effect of ties.

The correction factor is:

$$C^* = 1 - \frac{\sum_{i=1}^{e}(t_i^3 - t_i)}{(n_T^3 - n_T)}$$

Where: e = the number of different observations in the samples
t_i = the number of observations tied with the ith observation in size
n_T = the total number of responses in all samples

Then, W corrected = W/C^*

The test is the same as any comparison of means. Whenever the value of W corrected is greater than the Chi-squared table value at degrees of freedom (k-1) and the specified significance level, we reject the null hypothesis and conclude that the means differ. When W corrected is less than the table value, we conclude that the means are statistically equal. In other words, there is no reason to believe that the attributes differ in their ratings from a statistical perspective.

See Figure 4.1, which is a graph of the Chi-squared distribution showing the .05 significance level for the hypothesis test.

Once the conclusion is made that there is a difference in means, we conclude that the mean that stands out as the highest or lowest is the one that is statistically different.

Data Summary

When all the raw data were compiled, we calculated an "average satisfaction score" for each attribute to see whether we could notice any differences in perception reported by customers for each attribute.

On a scale of 1 to 10, with 1 being "Not at all Satisfied" and 10 being "Exceeded my Expectations," the average results are shown in Table 4.1.

This is the natural way we would choose to analyze the data. For the first-time respondents, the obvious outlier is price; a score of 6.8 is much lower than the other attribute scores. It would be easy to conclude that customers believe price is too high, resulting in the lowest satisfaction score among all the attributes. When looking at the first-time non-respondents, this conclusion is not so obvious. In fact, price did not stand out as much lower than the other attributes. In fact, it is higher than the score from first-time respondents.

The next step in the process is to conduct a formal analysis to study whether there is a difference based on the Kruskal-Wallis test. This analysis is summarized in Tables 4.2, 4.3, and 4.4. In Table 4.2, the raw satisfaction data is shown as the responses from five customer surveys on each of the

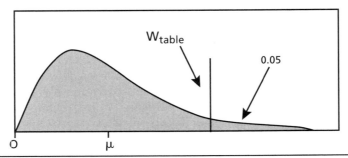

Figure 4.1 Chi-squared probability density function.

Comparing the Data (Rank Order Analysis)

Table 4.1 Respondent's average rating.

	First time	
	Respondents	Non-Respondents
Was everyone courteous?	9.4	9.4
Did we schedule a time that was convenient for you?	9.2	9.2
Did we arrive on time?	8.6	8.6
Was our price competitive?	6.8	8.4
Do you believe you received good value?	7.8	8.6

Table 4.2 Raw scores for responses from first time respondents.

	Courtesy	Convenient time	Arrive when promised	Competitive pricing	Value
Customer #1	10	9	9	7	8
Customer #2	9	9	9	8	8
Customer #3	10	10	9	6	7
Customer #4	9	8	8	7	8
Customer #5	9	10	8	6	8
Average satisfaction score	9.4	9.2	8.6	6.8	7.8

five questions, along with the average satisfaction scores. Table 4.3 segregates the data into a summary of scores by rating (the 1 to 10 scale). This permits us to calculate the "rank" of each response. Then, Table 4.4 combines the rating score for each customer and each attribute with the rank. By summing the ranks, we have a measure to use in the Kruskal-Wallis calculation of the test statistic, W.

54 Chapter Four

Table 4.3 Rank calculation for rating scores.

	# Observations		Rank
Lowest 1	0		—
2	0		—
3	0		—
4	0		—
5	0		—
6	2	1,2	1.5
7	3	3,4,5	4
8	8	6,7,8,9,10,11,12,13	9.5
9	8	14,15,16,17,18,19,20,21	17.5
Highest 10	4	22,23,24,25	23.5
	25		

Table 4.4 Sum of ranks analysis for first time respondents.

	Courtesy	Rank	Convenient time	Rank	Arrive when promised	Rank
Customer #1	10	23.5	9	17.5	9	17.5
Customer #2	9	17.5	9	17.5	9	17.5
Customer #3	10	23.5	10	23.5	9	17.5
Customer #4	9	17.5	8	9.5	8	9.5
Customer #5	9	17.5	10	23.5	8	9.5
Sum of ranks		99.5		91.5		71.5

	Competitive pricing	Rank	Value	Rank
Customer #1	7	4.0	8	9.5
Customer #2	8	9.5	8	9.5
Customer #3	6	1.5	7	4.0
Customer #4	7	4.0	8	9.5
Customer #5	6	1.5	8	9.5
Sum of ranks		20.5		42.0

Calculation for the test statistic, W:

$$W = \left[\frac{12}{n_T(n_T+1)} \sum_{i=1}^{k} \frac{R_i^2}{n_i}\right] - 3(n_T+1)$$

$n_T = 25$

$$W = \frac{12}{25 \times 26}\left[\frac{99.5^2}{5} + \frac{91.5^2}{5} + \frac{71.5^2}{5} + \frac{20.5^2}{5} + \frac{42.0^2}{5}\right] - 3(25+1)$$

$W = 0.01846\ [\ 1980.05 + 1674.45 + 1022.45 + 84.05 + 352.8\ ] - 78$

$W = 0.01846\ (5113.8) - 78 = 94.40 - 78 = 16.40$

Correction factor for ties

$$C^* = 1 - \frac{\sum_{i=1}^{e}(t_i^3 - t_i)}{(n_T^3 - n_T)} = 1 - \frac{[(2^3-2) + (3^3-3) + (8^3-8) + (8^3-8) + (4^3-4)]}{(25^3 - 25)}$$

$$= 1 - \frac{(6) + (24) + (504) + (504) + (60)}{15{,}600} = 1 - \frac{1098}{15{,}600}$$

$$= 1 - .07$$

$$= .93$$

$e = 5$ different observations in the samples
$t_1 = 2$ observations tied for the rank of 6
$t_2 = 3$ observations tied for the rank of 7
$t_3 = 8$ observations tied for the rank of 8
$t_4 = 8$ observations tied for the rank of 9
$t_5 = 4$ observations tied for the rank of 10

W corrected $= W/C^* = 16.4 / 0.93 = 17.63$

The table value of the Chi-squared distribution @ 95% confidence level and $k - 1 = 5 - 1 = 4$ degrees of freedom $= 9.488$

Conclusion, reject the null hypothesis. There is a statistically significant difference between the means.

56 Chapter Four

The test disproves equality of the means any time the calculated value of the test statistic (W corrected) is greater than 9.488. This is conclusive evidence that at least one of the attributes is statistically higher or lower than the other attributes. In the calculation of the value W corrected, we must evaluate the sum of the ranks for each attribute; that is, the measure of the composite score for each of the attributes. Price has the lowest rank measure of all the attributes, and it confirms the relative standing of price in the means of the attributes calculated earlier.

Kruskal-Wallis Conclusions for Initial Non-Respondents

We wanted further validation that price is a real concern to our customers. Recognizing that the sample of customer responses represented a healthy response rate of 20% of all surveys mailed, we know that 80% of the customer base did not send back surveys. We also know that first time respondents are usually customers with something very good or very bad to say. Initial non-respondents are in the "merely satisfied" category and usually have responses that are lower than the first-time respondents. By doing a parallel analysis of the initial non-respondents, we can estimate the rating of these attributes to a wider customer base. This is a way to confirm the conclusions we drew from the first-time respondents.

Tables 4.5 and 4.6 are examples of results for initial non-respondents, showing how their conclusions may differ from our initial group of survey respondents.

Table 4.5 Rank calculation for rating scores.

	# Observations		Rank
Lowest 1	0		—
2	0		—
3	0		—
4	0		—
5	0		—
6	0		—
7	0		—
8	8	1,2,3,4,5,6,7,8	4.5
9	13	9,10,11,12,13,14,15,16,17,18,19,20,21	15.0
Highest 10	4	22,23,24,25	23.5
	25		

Table 4.6 Sum of ranks analysis for first-time non-respondents.

	Courtesy	Rank	Convenient time	Rank	Arrive when promised	Rank
Customer #1	10	23.5	9	15.0	9	15.0
Customer #2	9	15.0	9	15.0	9	15.0
Customer #3	10	23.5	10	23.5	9	15.0
Customer #4	9	15.0	8	4.5	8	4.5
Customer #5	9	15.0	10	23.5	8	4.5
Average satisfaction score	9.4		9.2		8.6	
Sum of ranks		92.0		81.5		54.0

	Competitive pricing	Rank	Value	Rank
Customer #1	8	4.5	9	15.0
Customer #2	8	4.5	8	4.5
Customer #3	9	15.0	9	15.0
Customer #4	8	4.5	9	15.0
Customer #5	9	15.0	8	4.5
Average satisfaction score	8.4		8.6	
Sum of ranks		43.5		54.0

This group did not give us evidence that they thought price was an issue at the .05 significance level. The results show that for initial non-respondents, although price is still rated lower in customer satisfaction, the difference is not statistically significant when compared to the other attributes in contributing to customer satisfaction.

The calculations show, using the same analytical technique we used for the first-time respondents, that for initial non-respondents the value of W corrected at the .05 significance level and 8 degrees of freedom is W corrected = 7.636. The test disproves equality of the means anytime the value of the test statistic is greater than 9.488. In this case, initial non-respondents do not feel that price is an issue.

This conclusion is not obvious based on the average satisfaction scores. The formal analysis must be performed to evaluate this data. Our conclusion is that price is a motivator for some of the customers, but not for all.

Now that we know the statistical results, we must rely on the management team to construct a root cause analysis of the reasons for this price objection. (This will be covered in depth in Chapter 5.) The fact that first-time respondents and first-time non-respondents have different feelings about the company's performance in the price category is a complex problem. It points out the importance of making that extra effort to have first-time non-respondents fill out surveys and mail them in. They represent the majority of the customers and they often have different opinions about the company. In other words, they represent two different populations; each must be analyzed separately.

The process employed is the same one we can use for any study of customer satisfaction metrics. In summary:

- Ask customers what attributes are most important to them.

- Poll customers with current experience about the company's performance in these customer-identified attributes either continuously (once a month for all those who have had an experience with the company that month), or periodically (such as once a year).

- Perform a Kruskal-Wallis test on the customer satisfaction metrics for all the attributes to determine whether any show statistically significant differences.

- Check the consistency of those conclusions by including first-time non-respondents (representative of the remaining customer base) in the analysis.

- Present the results to the management team for development of strategic initiatives to deal with any statistically significant differences between attributes, within the context of the business plan and the customer's perception of customer satisfaction.

This process can be employed with any quality improvement program; it offers the confidence of a statistical basis to discriminate between attributes that need attention and those that will not result in measurable increases in customer satisfaction even if we improved them.

To be clear on this point, giving appropriate attention to an attribute should result in improvement. However, we may maximize our use of resources by concentrating on the attributes that are the lowest, those that offer the most return from our investments. Low attributes are often considered "deal-breakers" by customers who will not do business with companies that have very poor performance in an important attribute.

We often think we know what our customers want, but unless we ask them, we are never really sure. We often think we know what attributes our customers want us to improve, but if we work on the wrong ones (often those that are easiest for us to affect), we miss the opportunity to have a measurable, positive effect with our customers.

Notes

The Kruskal-Wallis method may be found in the text *Business Statistics in Practice,* Third Edition, Bowerman, O'Connell, McGraw Hill, 2003.

This chapter is adapted from the author's article "Using Statistics to Improve Satisfaction," *Quality Progress,* March 2007.

5
Methods Used to Find Underlying Causes

"Quality is never an accident; it is always the result of intelligent effort."

John Ruskin

SYSTEMS VERSUS UNDERLYING CAUSES

Consider lack of communication, a common cause of customer frustration. Many customers believe that their vendor is too slow to give them information or that it doesn't give them the information they really need. That is a symptom. The underlying cause might be a report that has not been developed or a service the customer is unwilling to purchase. One way to brainstorm for underlying causes is to use a cause-and-effect diagram, sometimes called a fishbone diagram for obvious reasons. Figure 5.1 is a generic fishbone diagram.

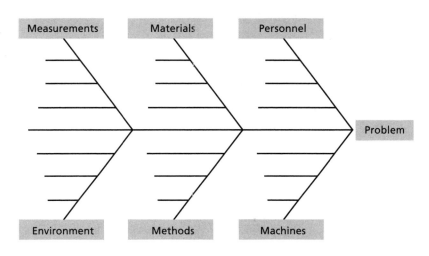

Figure 5.1 Generic fishbone diagram.

The symptom (problem to be solved) is at the head of the diagram on the extreme right side. The "fish bones" represent the major categories of underlying causes we could brainstorm as possible reasons for the problem. This is the time for uncensored ideas and opinions, no matter how unlikely the suggestion. Suspending practicality at this time fosters an atmosphere of free thinking; even an unlikely idea may spark a better idea from that person or someone else in the session. It is only when the creative juices have abated that we can take a more sober view of the probability of each of the underlying causes that are listed.

Let's take the example of poor customer communication and fill in some potential underlying causes for that problem.

Under the "Measurements" category we might have:
- Insufficient data accumulated to give the customer what they need, or
- Client unwilling to share their database with us, or
- Inaccuracy in our data gathering

Under the "Materials" category we might have:
- No identifiable cause

Under the "Personnel" category we might have:
- Employees not trained in customer service, or
- Insufficient personnel in the service department

Under the "Environment" category we might have:
- Time difference between New York and Paris causes issues, or
- The internet server we use is occasionally unreliable

Under the "Methods" category we might have:
- Our process to run those reports is done only once a day, at night, or
- The customer takes two days to distribute mail internally, or
- Information from the field is delayed getting to us until the next morning, or
- Service operators don't have access to that information

Under the "Machines" category we might have:
- We're switching e-mail servers and there are bugs to be worked out, or
- Service operators don't have access to that information

Some underlying causes may have several roots, or several ways we might look at solving the cause. Many of these broad categories may have six or more underlying causes we can identify. That is great. We don't have to use them all. In fact, later in this chapter we will look at finding the most likely causes of the problem as a place to start our journey of customer satisfaction improvement.

Usually, these broad underlying categories will capture all of your ideas. There may be times when one of these categories is not needed or your problem is so specific that you must add categories unique to your business. This is a tool and a framework, not a binding contract. Modify it to suit your needs. The only advice for using a fishbone diagram is not to confuse broad categories with specific underlying causes. The details should always lead to actionable events that have a chance of solving the business problem. We'll see how to do that when we review the method of the "Five Whys."

Underlying Causes That Result in "Real" Change versus Those That Don't

Just because an underlying cause is plausible doesn't mean it will result in measurable improvement. Alternatively, even when an underlying cause does improve the process and correct the problem in some ways, it may not be justified or even cost effective. When we seek a solution, our criteria should be:

1. Which potential solution will give me the most return? If one solution will give me an 80% improvement and another will give me 20%, I want to look at the solution that will give me the most as long as it also meets the second criterion.

2. Which solution(s) will cost us the least to implement? In many cases, analyzing the cost/benefit ratio is a step that is easily forgotten. We rarely do a complete evaluation of the financial impact of corrective action or continuous improvement projects because it is natural to grab at the solution that is least costly to implement (regardless of the benefit expected). The justification is that it doesn't affect the budget much and we can claim a real improvement (no matter how insignificant).

In many cases, the improvement that results in major benefits may cost us nothing or even save us money. An example would be the case toward the end of Chapter 2. The company saves money and the customer is better satisfied.

Five Whys

The fishbone diagram is a useful way to categorize root causes and focus our attention on specific areas for improvement. However, these ideas may not be deep enough to crystallize a solution to the problem. Enter the method called the *Five Whys*. Introduced by Toyota in the 1930s, this method is used by Six Sigma Green Belts and Black Belts to drill down into the root causes of issues to find the actionable item most likely to result in real change. The method requires us to ask "why" as many times as necessary to find the common denominator to our problem. Let's use our customer communication problem as an example. We started out with our fishbone diagram to get to the first stage of underlying cause. Here is the contribution of the Five Whys method.

Problem Statement: Symptom
Poor customer communication

Why #1: (From the "Personnel" category of the fishbone diagram)
"Because employees are not trained in customer service."

Why #2: Why are employees not trained in customer service?
"We do not have any formal training program."

Why #3: Why is there no formal training program?
"We use on-the-job training for those employees."

Why #4: Why is OJT not working?
"Some employees must be on the job for about a year in order to become acquainted with all customer needs."

Why #5: Why can't we acquaint employees with customers' special needs more quickly?
"Institute formal training in addition to 'On the Job Training' before putting the employee on the job by themselves."

When using this technique, it's important to answer each "why" question with facts and not speculation. In the next section, we will show how to shorten the list of suggested ideas to a few that have high potential for improvement in customer satisfaction. Asking "why" often uncovers other deeper and more basic underlying causes, and prompts us to ask another "why." The rule of thumb is that it takes five "whys" to get to the basis for our solution. We would do this for our suggested underlying causes in the fishbone diagram (that are chosen for final analysis) to be sure that we have the lowest level of improvement possibility and one that will address all the shortcomings uncovered by our "whys." In some cases it might take fewer than five "whys." In other cases, it might take more.

THE PLAN, DO, STUDY, ACT CYCLE

> *"If you cannot describe what you are doing as a process, you do not know what you are doing."*
>
> W. Edwards Deming

Now that we have our list of probable causes, we should spend some time shortening the list to those that have the highest probability of success. If we did our job well, we have facts on which to base our opinions about root causes. This may include wasted material cost, high labor cost, number of missed calls, or number of customer complaints.

One method we can use is to plot the opportunity for improvement by evaluating the cost of non-compliance or failure to meet satisfaction targets. Let's say we hypothesize that our lack of communication is based on too few personnel on the phones, lack of training for our operators in customer service, and calls coming in before our normal work day begins. All three are illustrated in our fishbone diagram study. We know that too few personnel on the phones results in a long customer wait-time on hold, costing us $30 per call. A lack of operator training results in transferred calls, angering clients because they don't have one-call service and costing us $20 per call. Lastly, inadequate service for European clients who call during their work day (early in the AM for Americans) costs us $150 per call in lost revenue. We can analyze this data to learn the most important reason to address this communication issue. If we accumulate this data, we might have a result such as that shown in Table 5.1.

A Pareto chart is a histogram that orders the causes of our problem from the highest number to the lowest number of observances. See Figure 5.2. In the first case, we are looking at the number of calls affected by poor service. It is clear that having too few personnel affects the largest number of client calls.

Now, let's look at a Pareto chart that includes the cost of each of these underlying causes. A different story emerges. In this chart, the underlying cause that results in the greatest lost revenue is missing calls before 8:00 a.m. Although that is the lowest number of observations, each incidence costs us much more than either inadequate personnel or lack of training. This Pareto chart is shown in Figure 5.3.

Table 5.1 Reason for poor communication.

Reason	Number of calls affected
Too few personnel	690
Lack of training	414
Calls before 8 a.m.	230
Reason	**Cost of poor customer service**
Calls before 8 a.m.	$34,500
Too few personnel	$20,700
Lack of training	$ 8,280

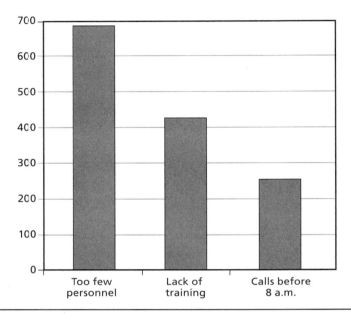

Figure 5.2 Number of calls affected.

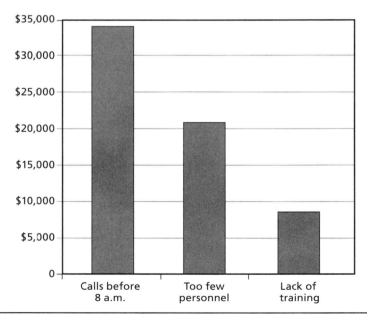

Figure 5.3 Cost of poor customer service ($).

We must be cautious when we find causes for our problem. It's possible to use the wrong analysis and work on an underlying issue that will not maximize lost revenue even though it addresses the largest number of complaints. It is always wise to look at cost to see whether that is the most compelling reason for addressing a problem.

Now it is time to review the scientific method. Under many names, the scientific method is a formulaic approach to problem solving. It involves the following:

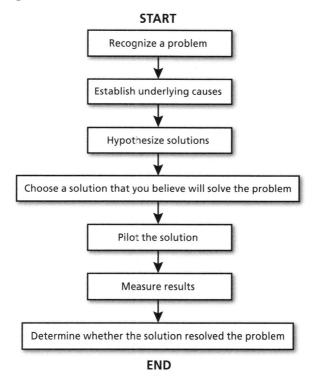

If the solution did not resolve the problem:

- Choose another solution that has been identified earlier.
- If no other solutions are identified, hypothesize additional solutions and start the pilot again.

If the solution resolves the problem in the pilot:

- Put the solution into practice
- Measure results to be assured that the solution is routinely applied and becomes practice.

In flowchart form, it looks like this:

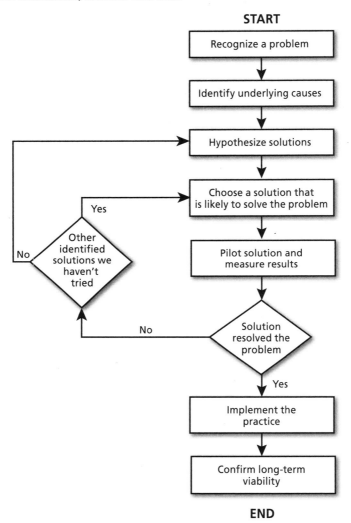

The DMAIC method is a Six Sigma approach used by many firms, including General Electric. The acronym stands for:
- Define
- Measure
- Analyze
- Improve
- Control

The Deming process uses a similar method called the Plan, Do, Study, Act cycle. This is illustrated in Figure 5.4.

All of these approaches seek to provide a template for the scientific method and a roadmap for taking a problem from the definition stage through to solution and confirmation of effectiveness. Whichever method we choose, we must pull together a team and lead them from the beginning to the end of the process until we have solved the original problem and can demonstrate that the solution is durable; that is, one that will be sustainable into the future.

Let's look at the Plan, Do, Study, Act cycle in more detail. In the first quadrant, the upper right quarter of the circle, we have the Plan activity. This is the part of the cycle where we define the problem, usually a symptom that is recognized as needing improvement. Using our running example, we see that improved communication with our customers might be identified as the first symptom to be addressed. At this point we should be thinking about the scope of this problem.

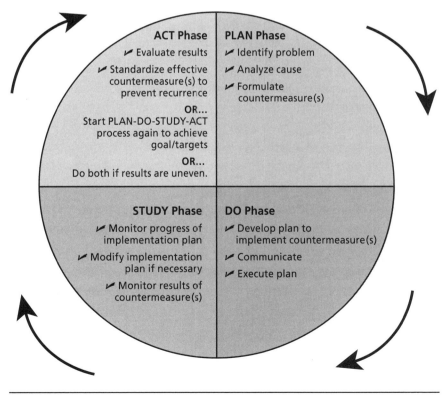

Figure 5.4 The Plan, Do, Study, Act cycle.

Before we go any further, let's consider our decision-making process. One of the tenets of *good* decision-making is that we should always act on the basis of facts and not guesses or intuition. Although there is a place for guessing in problem solving, notably in brainstorming potential root causes for a fishbone diagram, once we get into the mode of selecting the best root causes we should be doing that based on facts.

What is the actual number of missed calls in a month? How many customers say that communication is a problem? What is the estimated cost of a lost call? How have customer opinions of our ability to communicate changed over the last few years? What do our customers expect from our communications? What elements of communication are important to our customers (for example, newsletters, routine calls to see how things are going, notification of a problem with our system, and feedback about a new service or product we developed). Based on this information, can we identify the probable causes of our communication problem and which root causes have the most potential to result in improved communication? Perhaps there are several, because different customers define good communications differently.

Because planning is the most important part of many processes, we can now determine what changes might result in improved communication with customers. Perhaps a new newsletter. Perhaps quarterly meetings to review the program and provide an update on new services, including progress on any issues identified in the last quarter. Once we have identified things that are likely to improve communication, it is time to move on to the Do step.

In the second quadrant, the lower right quarter of the circle, we have the Do activity. In this part of the cycle, we will conduct a pilot experiment to test the impact of recommended solutions. We are interested in proving that our ideas for improvement will result in the changes we expected, at least on a limited scale.

The importance of these two activities, planning and doing, can't be overstated. If we haven't been rigorous in selecting probable root causes and demonstrating that those root causes have the potential to solve the problem, we can be mired in a never-ending loop of failure. When this happens, great solutions go undiscovered because we didn't do the brainstorming phase well. We have all been disappointed by evaluating solutions that just don't seem to be worthwhile. That is what happens when we don't have the right solutions test. We have all been surprised to learn that a solution we implemented doesn't solve the original problem. Equally disastrous, a solution has unintended consequences, rendering the solution worse than the original problem. If we are to start on the right path, we must pay extra attention to the discovery of potential solutions, find facts that confirm their correlation and causality with the original problem, and test the solution before implementing it broadly across the organization.

In the third quadrant, the lower left quarter of the circle, we have the Study activity. This activity involves examining the result of the pilot study to determine whether the process improvement has increased performance, as anticipated, for the problem we are studying. This is the evaluation phase where we look at the facts and see whether this is a solution we want to implement broadly. In addition, we see what we have learned about the relationship of the solution to the problem. Will this solution resolve 50% of our problem or more, are there additional costs associated with this solution that we hadn't considered, or are there consequences in other parts of the organization that are affected (good or bad) by this solution? This is the gatekeeper function, the go/no-go decision point.

If we have a good result from the pilot, we can make plans to administer the program throughout the operation. This will usually include changes in process documentation, employee training, and the insertion of new monitoring points to assure that the changes are durable. We are trying to avoid the all-too-frequent experience of putting in place a process change only to have the change ignored after a short time. If we affect every touch-point of the change by complete documentation, train employees in the new procedures, and measure compliance at regular intervals, we will better guarantee that the change will become a habit and a new part of our daily business.

If we don't have confirming evidence from the pilot, we will need to go back to the Plan stage of the cycle to find other underlying root causes to pilot. A failed pilot is not a bad result. It is much better to learn this lesson in the pilot than to find it once the new methods have been implemented at great cost throughout the organization, at which point we would have to backtrack and undo the changes we had implemented. It's necessary to go back to the drawing board looking for other potential solutions to our problem.

In the fourth quadrant, the upper left quarter of the circle, we have the Act activity. This activity focuses on taking what we have learned in the Study phase and implementing the best activities throughout the organization. This phase is characterized by the development of an implementation plan that includes people, resources, check points, and project timing. This is the time to write new procedures and standards. Training of employees, supervisors, and managers on the new procedures is a part of this phase, as is setting up monitoring of the consistent use and effectiveness of the changes.

Before we completely implement any solution, it's important to talk about whether these changes fit our mission and the direction we want to take the company. That is the topic of the next section.

DO THE AREAS NEEDING IMPROVEMENT PLAY TO OUR STRENGTHS?

"Change should be a friend. It should happen by plan, not by accident."

Philip Crosby

We can't be all things to all people. Sometimes customers ask us to do things that we don't want to do. They may cost too much to compensate for the benefit, they may take us out of our niche, or they may be a detriment to other customers. Good companies say "no" to customers when their requests do not fit the direction executives have strategized for the company. Strategies evolve as we define our market segments and the products and services we want to provide. This contributes to our corporate image or "branding."

A motor vendor I know discontinued making specialty motors for low-volume customers. These were high-profit products and represented a significant number of customers. However, the effort and investment to develop and produce the products constituted a high percentage of the vendor's cost of doing this business. One day the vendor sent a letter to all those low-volume customers saying that it would discontinue manufacturing those motors in nine months. They had decided to invoke the 80/20 rule and eliminate 80% of their customers while losing only 20% of their business. In this way they could concentrate on their high-volume customers. They were amenable to working with all their current low-volume customers, but they were adamant that they would cease shipping specialty motors in nine months.

Clearly, this decision was based on a business case that producing high-volume motors for only a few customers would permit the company to concentrate on its strengths. This decision should be made only when there is consistency between the corporate mission statement, the long-term strategic plan, the capital budget, and the annual operating plans. Each of these stages must be committed to this change of direction and the investment, consequences, and benefits should be studied before this decision is made. The strategy worked out fine for this vendor. Business increased and they were very profitable after making this decision.

Another case like this one involved a manufacturer who sold commercial products through manufacturers' representatives. They were having difficulty getting the attention of most of their rep organizations. These independent agents showed only lackluster interest in promoting the company's product lines. As independent business persons, manufacturers' reps don't take title to a product. They act as a middle-man to sell in a designated territory and they take a commission on the sale. A study revealed that the 80/20 rule was valid in this business as well. At least 80% of total sales were attributable to the work of 20% of the reps. Of the more than 350 reps who had rights to sell the products of this company, only about 80 of them accounted for more than 80% of total sales. The company decided to look over those territories with a more critical eye.

After a detailed analysis of each territory and the success of the reps in their regions, the company terminated sales agreements with about 225 rep organizations. That left about 125 rep companies where there had been 350. Each rep organization was given an exclusive territory to manage.

The benefits were:

- Fewer rep organizations to manage
- Reduced cost for training and the updating and distribution of materials
- Reduced turn-over in the sales force
- Reps weren't constantly arguing about exclusivity in their sales territories (four reps in one state might have overlapping territories, or one customer with offices and plants in 5 states might purchase from several locations, although sales agreements were signed in a central location.)
- Increased rep engagement in the product because of increased territory reach that was more in alignment with other product lines

Sales and profits for this manufacturer increased more than 50% in the next twelve months, illustrating that the changes fit the overall strategy of the organization. These two examples demonstrate that changes implemented well and supported throughout the organization can result in great success. The same conclusion can be drawn from customer satisfaction surveys.

The difference in the case of customer satisfaction surveys is that individual customer suggestions are often treated as insignificant and not worthy of being held up to the light of the company's mission, vision, or corporate strategy. That is far from correct. As an example, consider what would happen if we ran the motor company that so successfully fired most of its customers. A good high-volume customer needs a specialty motor for a special customer. Ten motors, that's all. One time. How much trouble can that be? Shouldn't we do everything we can for our high-volume customers? How does a request for 10 motors precipitate a check of our business direction? What are our options?

If we look at our mission statement, it will be clear that the request should not be honored. It doesn't play to our strengths, because we have structured our company around high-volume sales. The response to the customer is "No."

When we say "No" to a customer, we open the door to competitors. We encourage a customer to become acquainted with and purchase goods from our competitors. That is an invitation to lost business. But sometimes we have to say "No" because the request doesn't fit our business. We are faced with a problem common to anyone in business: How to say "No" but give the customers what they want. Actually, we have several options for solving this problem, but it is a business decision we should make as we anticipate this problem, not when we are confronted with it.

One potential solution is to make the motors in our model shop. Each will probably cost us ten to one hundred times the cost of a production motor, but it is an option. Another solution would be to have a relationship with a specialty motor manufacturer and simply place the order with them on behalf of your client. You can find even more creative ways to say "No" while saying "Yes" without compromising the mission of the company. Clearly, stopping the presses to manufacture these specialty motors on production equipment would be unattractive from a cost standpoint and would surely result in missed deliveries to your regular customers.

Any time a customer requests that you provide something you don't provide now, it is prudent to check the request against your mission and be certain that this is a direction you want to take the company.

Now let's look at requests that result in improvements to a delivery system or products. A graphic may help us understand the importance of comparing customer requests to our delivery system. Table 5.2 illustrates the relationship of performance versus the importance of attributes in the eyes of our customers.

We usually perform well in those areas in which we have a commitment in our mission and vision statements, as long as we are genuine in our intent and actions, and we reward all employees for measured success in those areas. Let's say that we have an active and successful program that meets the goals of our mission and vision. Then, when customers ask for change in a process, we should look first at the combination of performance and importance of the request.

Table 5.2 Performance – importance analysis.[1]

	Performance Low	Performance High
Importance Low	Who cares?	Overkill
Importance High	Vulnerable	Strengths

Requests that play to our strengths are those that have high importance to our customers and those that we perform well. Any request in this quadrant should be studied with a serious consideration to comply. These are the identified business opportunities in our "sweet spot," areas of core competencies, that permit internal growth. The next attractive opportunity is something we do well but that doesn't have much importance to our customer. This is the request we can honor easily and customers will be delighted.

The next opportunity involves attributes that are important to our customers in areas that don't play to our strengths. These represent opportunities for our competitors, and we risk encouraging customers to shift those requests to our competitors. As with the earlier example about specialty motors, when a special request has high importance to a good customer in an area that no longer plays to our strengths, we need a good solution. We might:

1. Start up a specialty motor operation for low-volume production outside the mainstream plant
2. Purchase a specialty motor company
3. Develop a relationship with an outsourcing vendor

We must be prepared with a prepackaged solution for customers who have requests related to our business but not playing to our strengths. In this way, we develop a strength where none existed before. That is a growth opportunity. We should simply decline requests that have low priority to our customers and also don't play to our strengths. We can't be all things to all people.

OVERCOMING RESISTANCE TO CHANGE

"It is not necessary to change. Survival is not mandatory."
                                          W. Edwards Deming

The Cause of Resistance

People resist change. However, if we want to improve customer satisfaction, we often have to do something different. The continuous improvement process is all about continuous "change." One definition of insanity is doing the same thing over and over but expecting a different outcome. If we want to implement a new process, then we must find a way to overcome peoples' natural resistance to change.

Let's recap where we are. We measured customer satisfaction and solicited comments about what we can do that will improve customer satisfaction. We took that information and decided which suggestions make most sense for us; we believe that if we improve particular attributes it will result in measurable improvement in customer satisfaction. Then we completed a root cause analysis to find the underlying cause(s) of the problem, and we hypothesized solutions that will resolve the problem. Now it is time to put that solution in place and measure whether it actually works. As we implement the solution, we are met with an obstacle: People resist the very change we worked so hard to develop.

In the parlance of decision-making, the easiest decision to make is a choice between two alternatives that results in a win-lose decision. All else being the same, and for the sake of simplicity, if faced with winning $100 or losing $20, we will take winning $100 every time and be happy about it.

The next easiest decision to make, one that gives us a bit more of a challenge, is the win-win decision. We must decide which option results in the bigger win. It may take some doing to find out which win results in the $100 payout rather than the $5 payout. If you don't think that a win-win decision is fraught with tension, just watch the game shows on TV that tempt players to choose boxes, each of which holds a different amount of money. Once we realize that none of the boxes contains a negative amount, we can understand the concept of choosing the least desirable box based on the amount of money it contains, even though it results in a win for the contestant.

The hardest decision to make is the lose-lose decision. Both options offer a loss. It is hard to make a choice that will result in loss, even though we will intelligently make the choice that minimizes our loss. As an example, consider a customer lawsuit over the failure of your product to perform. All of your arguments have been ignored by the customer and their attorney: The product was misused, it was applied during inappropriate conditions by unqualified personnel, it was past its expiration date at the time of application, and any protection the company provides is expressed in the warranty, which had expired by the time the product was finally used. Now you are faced with a lawsuit.

You have two choices. Go forward with discovery and fight the suit, which will certainly cost the company lots of money, or settle out of court, giving up at least a modicum of integrity and pride to minimize your losses. Which would you happily choose? People resist process change on the job because they feel a sense of loss. In some way their world will change, taking them into a different future. They know that the proposed change is supposed to result in an improvement for the company, but they are thinking about themselves and how the change will affect them. In their minds, the promised gain is uncertain, but the loss of familiarity looms large before them.

Reaction to Change Agents[2]

The reaction felt by employees confronted by a need to change is driven by the perception of loss in at least one of these categories:

- *Security* – An uncertain future
- *Competence* – The need to learn something new
- *Relationships* – The potential need to belong to a new group and lose old colleagues
- *Sense of direction* – Change in mission
- *Territory* – Change of psychological or physical space

When confronted with a loss, employees go through a four-stage process in dealing with the change. These steps are:

- *Denial* – Believing that this phase will go away, that ignoring the change will hasten its demise.
- *Resistance* – An active effort to thwart the change by speaking and acting against efforts to further develop or implement the change.
- *Exploration* – Beginning to internalize the future; becoming creative in envisioning the new environment and how to structure themselves and the new process to be acceptable. This can be a chaotic time for individuals and the teams on which they contribute.
- *Commitment* – Teamwork begins to take hold, a clear focus and future are conveyed, and full implementation is begun.

Managers and leaders of organizations must put in place a process that engages employees in change with the minimal amount of stress. This means setting up continuous improvement processes that incorporate an understanding of the trauma of change and working with the employees to accept change as constructive and good for them. The Rogers Adoption/Innovation Curve looks like a normal distribution and identifies the five types of people in any organization (see Figure 5.5). They are:

1. Innovators
2. Early adopters
3. Early majority
4. Late majority
5. Laggards

In this model, there are two needs. The first is to get buy-in from the innovators and early adopters at the very start of the process. This drags the curve to the left, to earlier start times. The second is to begin the process

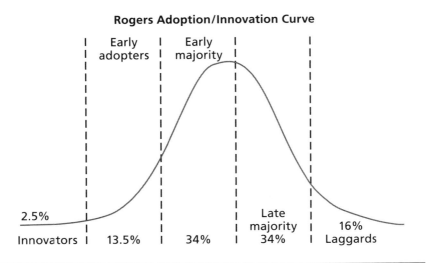

Figure 5.5 The five types of people in any organization.

of getting the masses to accept change a little earlier. The Rogers model presumes that it is useless to "quickly and massively convince the mass" of the need for substantive change. This leaves us with the only option that works, which is to work with the majority to shift the curve slightly to the left (earlier in time) with more of the early and late majority adopting sooner in the process.

The rationale for pulling the timeframe forward is that speed is a competitive advantage. The earlier a new product, service, or improvement is introduced, the more likely that the company will enjoy greater sales or greater cost reduction for a longer period of time. We want our competitors to play catch-up, not us.

Change management is a study in itself. This chapter talks about change from the standpoint of a project manager handling a team to implement change in the organization. The process has its roots in Six Sigma training where continuous change is the norm. Six Sigma Black Belts are well trained in working with groups to sensitize them to rapid change and to understand and work within the dynamic of a constantly changing environment (continuous improvement organization). The very basic model of change requires employees to:

Because of our predisposition to hold on to the familiar, it takes an effort to let go of the past. Once we are convinced that change is in our best interest, which can take some doing, we are ready to investigate the way our future might look once the change is in place. This is the transition phase where we get comfortable with the *prospect* of change. Finally, we step into the commitment phase where we engage in the change activity. Through repetition, we form new habits and a new familiar pattern for the future.

This can be summarized as an eight-stage process:[3]

1. Establish a sense of urgency
2. Create the guiding coalition
3. Develop a vision and strategy
4. Communicate the vision
5. Empower broad-based action
6. Generate short-term wins
7. Consolidate the gains to produce more change
8. Anchor new approaches in the culture

To accomplish this process, we must charter a group of employees who can make it happen. Their characteristics should include a strong bias for action and a comfort level with risk. Why risk? Any change has a chance of not meeting its goals. When employees (or teams) become paralyzed by failure, which is not a good trait for a continuous improvement team, they are not effective nor do they meet their goals. The team should be populated with participants who can recognize failure for what it is, a message that what we tried didn't work. Failure is just another indicator that the program must be redirected. Failing gives us important information about what does not work, which helps us to find the direction that will result in success.

After spending years on research and thousands of failed experiments to build a prototype of the light bulb, Edison was asked by a reporter if he was discouraged. He said that he had not failed. He had successfully discovered thousands of ways not to build a light bulb! That is the kind of attitude we want in our team members.

Structuring the Organization for Continuous Improvement

When we are ready to establish the team that will implement change as defined by our customers, we can follow the process that is well known to Six Sigma organizations. First, we must choose a leader for the team and encourage a learning organization for the team members. The underlying reason for creating a culture of education and training is that people must know what to do and how to do it.

In this context, a learning process will incorporate both education and training. In Deming's 14 points he distinguishes between these two. Education is intended to make people smarter. This helps the organization by fostering an environment where critical thinking is the norm. A good education process is one that does more than just fill student heads with information. It is a process within which information is presented; students must assimilate that knowledge into applications that show a detailed understanding of the implications of the content, and integration of the content, into problems. It is not simply knowledge of the terminology or definitions.

Training is something different. Training is practical information that permits you to go back to your job and demonstrate a new or improved skill. It makes you smarter in a focused, job-oriented way rather than broadly increasing critical thinking skills. Clearly, our team must know what to do (critically evaluating ideas and engaging problem-solving methods) and how to do it (demonstrating skill in operations, implementation, and measurement). Good leadership is another topic entirely.

Are leaders born, or are they nurtured through good mentoring and learned experiences? While there are arguments on both sides of this question, we think that at least some of the skills needed to lead teams can be taught. There are certainly enough Organizational Leadership programs at the college level to cause us to believe at least some of the management and leadership skills can be taught. It might be instructive to review the differences between management and leadership attributes summarized in Table 5.3.

Table 5.3 The differences between management and leadership attributes.

Managers	Leaders
Doing things right	Doing the right things
Establishing procedure	Creating a vision for the future
Setting budgets and resources	Strategizing change agents
Creating structure	Creating empowered teams and coalitions
Delegating responsibility and authority	Reinforcing the mission and vision
Monitoring results	Breaking down bureaucratic barriers to reinforce a culture of success
Solving problems	Providing empathetic support for all employees
Delivering on time	Staying on budget
This demonstrates:	
Predictability and order	Environment that welcomes change
Consistency	Pro-activity

In this model, managers are concerned with functional deployment of activities and leaders prepare the organization and its employees for an environment of change. The team leader's responsibility is to create a dynamic group that can excite itself and the employees of the organization to reach for continuous improvement. This isn't a one-time change, but rather a commitment to continuous change. The more people who are engaged in the change process, the more buy-in they will project and the greater success that will be achieved in the company. A four-stage model is used to characterize the establishment of any team:

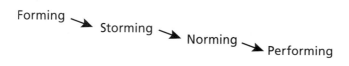

When a team is *Forming*, the team members are getting to know each other, their strengths and weaknesses, and their motivation to contribute to the team's efforts. This is the time to select team members who have a bias for change and performance. The members should be motivated intrinsically and work hard to accomplish the goals of the organization because they enjoy success. Getting the bus going in the right direction is critically important, but having the right people on the bus is equally important.

When the team is *Storming*, we experience a chaotic period of team-building. Members are jockeying to be accepted as an expert in an area of expertise, exerting individuality, and competing for recognition. The leader must let this process progress, but control the team so that it does not become destructive. The end result of this stage is to carve out responsibilities and to establish the rules of conduct. This is the time to recognize team members who were chosen in error, who don't fit the requirements of the team, or who can't get along and make necessary changes. Not much work progress gets done in this stage.

When the team is *Norming*, it is starting to work together toward a common goal. Roles are aligned and relationships are formed. Members share information and work constructively. There is cohesiveness within the group and they listen to one another. They are finally prepared to work efficiently.

When the team is *Performing*, members are making decisions for the betterment of the team and the project. There is a high level of cooperation and output. Ideas are being tested and analyzed.

Finally, we have overcome the resistance to change and we are structured to make real progress on continuous improvement.

Notes

1. From *The Management and Control of Quality,* 5th Ed, James R. Evans, 2002, South-Western/Thomson Learning.
2. From *Managing Change at Work,* Cynthia D. Scott & Dennis T. Jaffe, 1995, Crisp Publications.
3. Adapted from Kotter, "Why Transformation Efforts Fail," *Harvard Business Review* (March-April 1995): 61.

6

Setting Improvement Objectives and Customer Satisfaction Goals

"Quality is the result of a carefully constructed cultural environment. It has to be the fabric of the organization, not part of the fabric."

Philip Crosby

It doesn't matter where we start, as long as we have an appropriate goal for continuous improvement. The first step is to find out how we are perceived by our customers. Once we decide to measure customer satisfaction, it is not productive to be disappointed in our ratings or the esteem in which we are held by our customers. The purpose of seeking customer feedback is to help us improve, not to punish ourselves over our current relative standing. Seeking feedback and complaints from our customers, as highlighted in Chapters 2 and 3, gives us the ammunition we need to plan our improvement goals.

After all, what would happen if we consistently asked our customers how we could improve and we chose action items directed at improving customer satisfaction each year? What would happen if every time we found a product defect we improved the design of the product (or the manufacturing process or the component parts) to the point where we had a product that met our profit margins and our customer expectations? We would have a company that truly acted on the advice of our customers and we would enjoy high levels of customer satisfaction. In fact, finding problems should not be viewed negatively. Finding problems means finding opportunities for improvement.

How do we set improvement objectives? One action we must take is to measure the attributes we want to improve. We can't improve something that we can't measure. A second action is to dedicate resources to the project. A company I know set a goal to reduce the product cost for its highest volume product. This product cost the company $100 to produce; it set as its goal an annual $5 cost reduction. This was the company champion's most important job. At the beginning of each year, accounting, reliability, purchasing, manufacturing, and other departments identified team contacts who were responsible for any contributions needed for the project. The employees working on this project were well known throughout the company and their goal was widely publicized. The project valued cost avoidance as well cost reductions. For example, if a component part was expected to increase in price by $0.20 and the team brought it down to $0.15, they could count the $0.05 savings as part of the cost reduction. If they found another vendor to provide the part for an increase of just $0.05, they could claim the $0.15 savings. They had unlimited access to internal resources for the evaluation of design or manufacturing changes, but they had a strict capital budget. The team reported year-to-date results monthly. Their efforts were recognized at an awards ceremony each year, and their absence would have been obvious. In my five years at the company, they never failed to meet their goal.

That begs the question, "Was the goal set too low?" And that leads to deeper questions about the meaning of goals and the motivation that is created by setting goals.

When goals are set too low, we usually meet them. This may be motivating, but it doesn't result in the best outcome for the company. A certain amount of challenge should be attendant in reaching goals. When goals are set too high, we never reach them. Some managers believe that setting goals just out of reach will drive employees to put out more effort. In fact, it often has the opposite result. Instead of creating ever greater returns as employees press for greater gains, this technique destroys motivation. When employees who are working hard fail to achieve impossible goals, they stop trying.

Effective goals must be based on several criteria:

- Attainable: most of the time

- Specific: a known, measurable outcome that is recognized when achieved

- Mutually agreed upon: by management and the employee or team

Simply saying "Do the best you can!" is not a clear goal, although it might be welcome by some employees. It is almost impossible to fail in achieving that goal; no matter where you end up, it can be interpreted as the "best" you can do, all things considered. Let's consider the low goal as represented in Figure 6.1.

In this case, we have a low goal and a deadline to achieve it. Research shows that as we approach our goals, we slow down our efforts and experience a diminished marginal return as we get closer to the deadline. We reach the goal very near the deadline because the goal is no longer motivational to us. Other goals become important and we redirect our efforts to other more pressing activities. There is little satisfaction in achieving low goals; it becomes a matter of simply ticking off another task that must be accomplished. If this low goal is rewarded in a way that is outsized to our perceived effort, we become confused by the inequity and expect to receive accolades every time we do mundane tasks. This sets the wrong values to promote superior performance in the future.

Now let's say we overcompensate for this poor goal-setting by setting goals so outrageously high that we never achieve them. This is represented as an overlay in Figure 6.2.

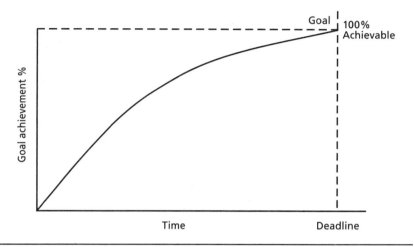

Figure 6.1 Low achievable goal.

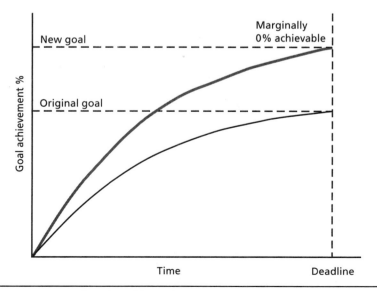

Figure 6.2 Marginally achievable goal.

In this case, we never achieve the goal because it is out of reach. People who consistently fail to reach goals stop trying; they recognize that success is not to be found in this endeavor and they move on.

Good goals lie somewhere between these two extremes. Figure 6.3 shows this value, but exactly where should we place this goal?

In goal-setting parlance we refer to goals that are within reach but that require hard work as "stretch" goals. Those are the most satisfying goals for most employees. In fact, a good standard is to reach 80% of your goals and come close to the rest. This standard provides sufficient motivation to succeed and enough stress to require thoughtful effort. Matching meaningful rewards to achievement of goals creates a motivating work environment.

We use our experience to decide where that goal should be. Sometimes we will be too high and other times too low, partly because of conditions that are outside of our control. What are some methods that could help us to set meaningful goals?

SMART Goal Setting

To expand on our previous criteria, we could use the SMART method of goal setting. This stands for:

    S = Specific
    M = Measurable
    A = Attainable
    R = Realistic
    T = Timely

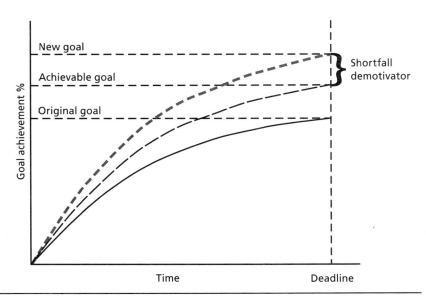

Figure 6.3   Stretch goals.

This goal does not meet the SMART criteria: "I plan to lose some weight."

This goal does meet the SMART criteria: "I plan to lose five pounds in the next month."

Specific: Since we can't change or control something we can't measure, every team should strive to set goals that have a stated outcome. We need to know when we have achieved the goal. If we lose a single pound, we will have achieved the letter of the goal, but not its desired outcome.

Measureable: If the goal can't be measured, we won't know when we have reached it. If we don't have a scale, how can we tell when we reach our goal of losing five pounds, or even measure our progress over time? If we can't see the difference between successful outcome and failure, we will likely accept poor performance, which we would objectively view as failure.

Attainable: This is the knowledge that the goal can be achieved. Most people eventually stop working on goals that are unachievable; our subconscious keeps us from wasting our time.

Realistic: This is closely related to the attainable attribute. However, just because goals are attainable, that doesn't mean they are realistic. We don't want to set low expectations to achieve realism, we want something that is not only attainable but motivating. We can see progress early, and it moves us to achieve higher performance.

Timely: Achieving a goal when the benefits can no longer help the organization is the same as a failure. If we need to introduce a new product this year in order to scoop the market, or if we need a cost reduction this month to protect our profit margins and these goals are realized next year, we have not met our goals because the temporal factor has not been achieved. It is too late to provide the needed benefits. Telling a child to clean up a room but failing to give a time frame leaves it up to the child to decide when the work should be done. Telling a child to clean up the room before 6:00 PM tonight provides a time frame. That timeframe may be negotiable, but it is not uncertain. The motivational time frame also must be attainable and realistic.

One approach to understanding the scope of the problem is to think about your vision for a perfect result. That becomes the definition of the goal and everything else is details. Now let's attack the details. What must you accomplish in order to achieve the vision of a perfect result? Make a list of all the things you must complete before the vision is realized. It's like making a shopping list for grocery items you must purchase before you can realize that wonderful dinner you envision. It also starts you thinking of the order of actions that must be followed before the end result is achieved. Not only do we have a to-do list, we have a flowchart of the actions necessary to reach our goal.

Setting Objectives

The vision is the first step in goal setting. After that, we want to take those action items and set intermediate objectives. In other words, we must establish the detailed plan to get from where we are to where we envision we want to be. This requires answering a number of questions:

- Who will do each task?
- What role will they play?
- What do we expect of each participant on the team?
- What authority will each team member have?
- What outside resources will we need?
- Does the team need training to understand the problem or solution techniques?
- How will we perform periodic reviews of performance?
- What are the measures of success?
- What are the tangible and intangible obstacles to our success? Be honest. Not everyone has the same vision we do, and some people are willing and able to limit our success.
- Can our success contribute to the individual performance metrics of each team member?

Rewards for Achieving the Goal

Another dimension of goal setting is the assignment of a reward once the goal is reached. For those who diet, it is often said that there should be a reward for reaching the goal. Many believe that pizza or ice cream (choose the item you would miss most) is a good reward for having lost weight and reached a monthly goal. In fact, a new pair of pants or a new sweater is a better reward for having achieved a weight-loss goal. So too will we appreciate reaching the goal if we know there is a reward attached to its successful completion. Rewards are most effective when they are given to the team that reached the goal as well as to individuals for their personal contributions to the effort. To be most effective, rewards should be made public and identified as important to the organization.

MAKING IT HAPPEN TAKES A HIGH-LEVEL CHAMPION

"Quality means doing it right when no one is looking."

Henry Ford

People accomplish what the boss wants or what they are incented to accomplish. People are motivated by either intrinsic feelings or extrinsic rewards. Employees often experience intrinsic motivation for a job that is done out of love. You've heard employees say that they would "do anything" for a manager because their efforts were really appreciated.

Let's take this test. You are approached by a competitor of your employer and asked if you would like to interview for a job. What would you say?

"I'm flattered by this invitation, but...I'm not interested. Here, my manager treats me with respect, I am acknowledged for doing a good job, and I am given all the resources, support, and training I need. My job is being constantly enriched in ways that improve my ability to learn, expand, and help the company at higher levels. I am paid fairly and I have good benefits. My manager and employer understand my need to have balance in my life and they encourage me to pursue outside interests that include my family, because they know that when extra effort is needed occasionally, I will step up for the company. I am informed about how my contribution affects our customers and I'm informed about how the company is doing. That helps me understand how I am progressing toward my incentive compensation. Given that, what can you offer me that is better than what has already been demonstrated by my current employer? I'd be taking a big chance going with you!"

That is an example of an environment that supports employees and has them eager to work and achieve important goals for the company. Now that we have a ready and willing workforce, why do we need management support?

Two varieties of management support exist for any major program, and both are involved in the complexities of improving customer satisfaction. The first is support from the CEO, sometimes referred to as a deployment champion.

If the top dog isn't behind the program, it will never happen. This is a broad statement to highlight the point that everything in the company emanates from the power wielded by the chief executive. The CEO specifies the mission and vision of the company. If the company mission statement doesn't reference quality processes or customer satisfaction in some way, it doesn't have great importance to the organization. The CEO approves budgets for all departments. If there is no money for quality initiatives, then people will not be assigned to projects directed at quality improvement, and money can't be spent on quality programs. Without the CEO strongly behind the quality program, it will not happen. With CEO support, money can be allocated, personnel will be assigned to the projects, and bonus and incentive payments can be made for meeting quality and customer satisfaction goals.

A company I know set annual performance objectives for its Product Planners that required project teams. These teams were formed from different functional areas in the company such as production, accounting, engineering, reliability, and purchasing to achieve company goals. Although important to the company's success, none of the functional areas was funded to support these projects. Product Planners were forced to cajole managers for resources in personnel, prototypes, and expenses to accomplish their goals. The direction was forthright, but the commitment was not consistent throughout the organization. While Product Planners were evaluated based on their performance in these projects, none of the managers or assignees was incented to work on the projects or fund resources to assure project success. Was this an oversight or simply a lack of consistent planning and commitment on the part of the CEO? Because it happened every year despite the discussion each year, it was probably a lack of commitment by the CEO. Some goals were met and others were not met. This was fine with the CEO, but not motivational for the Product Planners. There was significant turnover in that job function.

This brings up the second type of support critical to the success of any quality initiative: the personnel assigned (and funded) to engage in quality-related projects. These may be referred to as functional champions. In larger companies that take quality initiatives seriously, there are Master Black Belts, Black Belts, Green Belts, and other workers part of Six Sigma project teams whose directive is to save money for the company, improve quality, or both.

This terminology may be new to some readers. In general, employees with Master Black Belts supervise several employees who have attained the rank of Black Belt. Master Black Belts have training in project management, implementation, team building, and problem solving. They use tools such as statistical analysis and the scientific method and they have passed a rigorous exam demonstrating their skills in this arena. They spend time supervising Black Belts and they also provide training for other personnel in the organization who are engaged in quality initiatives.

Black Belts engage much more on building the teams and managing the projects and the performance of those who do the project work for the defined quality initiatives. Green Belts are employees who manage smaller projects and small teams with full responsibility for results as well. Black Belts and Green Belts are trained in quality processes and are often certified by exam. Most of the teams have employees who conduct the work under the guidance of the certified quality professionals. They are also trained in quality initiatives.

Larger companies can afford, and the scope of their projects need, one or several Master Black Belts to supervise the various major projects managed by the Black Belts. In smaller companies with smaller projects, Black Belts or even Green Belts can be tasked with the responsibility and authority to carry out quality-related projects.

Employing these highly specialized, professional quality experts represents an appreciable cost in personnel and training. It also represents a commitment up front, before any real savings or results of the quality improvement projects can be realized. There must be a high-level commitment to the quality process or this funding will never be made available.

In his book *Quality is Free,* Crosby tempts us to consider the prospect that quality efforts will more than compensate for their costs. In other words, quality needs funding, often a sizable investment, but once it begins to deliver cost savings, increased customer satisfaction, and higher sales, the benefits of the quality initiative will far exceed its costs. In that respect, it is free. In fact, once we net out the expenses for a quality operation from the increased revenue and decreased costs directly attributable to quality efforts, we will have a surplus of funds resulting in increased profits.

Getting Started Strategy

First, add a commitment to quality to the company mission statement. Show that customer satisfaction is a prime mover for the company, its policies, and its processes. Next, create some excitement for quality initiatives amongst the top management team. Then, take on a small project and accomplish it quickly to demonstrate that quality initiatives can be successful and profitable. The language of management is money. Convert success into monetary terms to make it attractive to management.

Lastly, ask for funding for a larger program, set objectives for continuous improvement (more on this in Chapter 8), involve all employees in the quality process, and enjoy the rewards of increasing customer satisfaction and business success.

Note

Find information on SMART goal setting from the website www.goal-setting-guide.com.

7
Implementation

"The quality of life is determined by its activities."

Aristotle

Now we actually have to do it! We know what our customers want and we have evaluated which projects we will accomplish. What are the steps we should take to improve customer satisfaction?

STEP 1: PUT A PLAN ON PAPER

This is the first step in establishing a commitment. A plan is more than a statement of goals. It explicitly describes the details of activities to better assure task success. For example, let's say that customers want more communication with the company, especially as it relates to new company offerings and important issues that will affect them immediately. The company's plan might be to initiate two new communication vehicles. Let's use this example to demonstrate an implementation process.

Scheduled Communications

One method of scheduled communication may be a monthly or quarterly newsletter that is emailed to all customers with an update on products and services. Some company activities are quite dynamic and require unscheduled communication, for example to announce signing a new customer, which can be broadcast by e-mail or text messaging immediately to all employees, customers, or other stakeholders. Another solution to the long-term communication issue, for companies that have relatively few customers, is to engage in quarterly in-person updates with the client. This is often referred to as a "balanced scorecard" update and includes a short presentation on:

Financial results: Specifically as they relate to the business conducted with this particular client, such as sales by product line and trends over time.

Customer relationship: A discussion of the working relationship and any modifications that the customer would like to see implemented in the future. It's important to set a timeline for the accomplishment of tasks identified by the customer. This becomes the front-and-center topic of conversation at the next scheduled customer meeting, including an update on progress that the company has achieved toward the goals.

Learning and growth: How is the company poised to change in the future, and what prospects will that have for the customer? What initiatives will be engaged to transform the company into a better partner? This differs from modifications specifically requested by customers to correct or improve the working relationship immediately. Learning and growth are transformative processes. Quarterly updates may not be necessary, but occasional updates may be used as a springboard for long-term planning with your customer.

Internal business processes: An update on the continuous improvement efforts necessary to streamline the company's procedures and set higher targets for efficiency and productivity.

For more information about the balanced scorecard strategic planning and management system, visit The Balanced Scorecard Institute at www.balancedscorecard.org.

The balanced scorecard system can be used as part of the Baldrige Criteria of "Management by Fact" or part of the ISO 9000 certification criteria of "Fact-Based Decision-Making." It is relevant to the implementation of continuous improvement projects. As an example, let's look at the Baldrige Award and its place in customer satisfaction.

Here is what the 2009-2010 Baldrige Criteria has to say about "Management by Fact:"

Management by Fact

"Organizations depend on the measurement and analysis of performance. Such measurements should derive from business needs and strategy, and they should provide critical data and information about key processes, outputs, and results. Many types of data and information are needed for performance management. Performance measurement should include customer, product, service, and process performance; comparisons of operational, market, and competitive performance; supplier, workforce, partner, cost, and financial performance; and governance and compliance outcomes. Data should be segmented by, for example, markets, product lines, and workforce groups to facilitate analysis.

Analysis refers to extracting larger meaning from data and information to support evaluation, decision making, improvement, and innovation. Analysis entails using data to determine trends, projections, and cause and effect that might not otherwise be evident. Analysis supports a variety of purposes, such as planning, reviewing your overall performance, improving operations, accomplishing change management, and comparing your performance with competitors' or with "best practices" benchmarks.

A major consideration in performance improvement and change management involves the selection and use of performance measures or indicators. *The measures or indicators you select should best represent the factors that lead to improved customer, operational, financial, and ethical performance. A comprehensive set of measures or indicators tied to customer and organizational performance requirements provides a clear basis for aligning all processes with your organization's goals. Measures and indicators may need to support decision making in a rapidly changing environment. Through the analysis of data from your tracking processes, your measures or indicators themselves may be evaluated and changed to better support your goals."*

The Baldrige Award is administered by the National Institute of Standards and Technology (NIST), an agency of the U. S. Department of Commerce. Companies are encouraged to apply for the award.

This statement in the Baldrige Guidelines is important because it leads us to find relevant criteria for the balanced scorecard we maintain for our customers. Each scorecard will be customized, based on measurable facts that we present to customers as an indicator of performance and continuous improvement. Information on the Baldrige Criteria may be found at www.quality.nist.gov.

The Baldrige Award Compared to ISO 9001:2008 Certification

The Baldrige Award is a competitive process by which examiners choose the best company in each category. Just as with the Academy Awards, where judges must choose the best picture in a given year, the quality of the other Baldrige applicants in any particular year will be a factor in whether a company wins.

Once a company has won the Baldrige award, it has that distinction forever. There is no requirement to maintain performance from year-to-year. The award cannot be taken away. Prior winners may not apply for the award every year.

The Baldrige Criteria are sometimes used by companies that have no intention of ever actually applying for the award. They consider the Baldrige Criteria and process to be a model of quality sustainability. These companies conduct an annual evaluation of their business to these standards to self-assess progress of the company toward higher performance.

In sharp contrast to this, ISO 9001:2008 is a certification. Companies must submit to an external audit periodically (perhaps every two years or so) in order to maintain certification. Certification may be rescinded if the company doesn't meet the continuing criteria for documented performance and improvement. This highly motivational process keeps a company on its best behavior year after year.

Unscheduled Communications

The second, more urgent communication vehicle is a real-time notice of issues that impact the customer. For example, an emergency notification is sent to all customers affected by a systems outage. In the service industry, customers want updates on the status of their repair orders. When I interview clients as part of my consulting business, I find that they always want more communication in the form of updates from their service providers.

In the Information Systems (IS) service business, clients feel lost without their computers. They want service to begin immediately and they want their computers back up and running quickly if there is ever a failure of any kind. Unfortunately, time is a relative concept. Talking to an interesting person for ten minutes may seem like just a few seconds; a few seconds touching a hot stove seems like an hour. Waiting for your computer to be restored to use is one of those events that seems to take much longer than the actual time of recovery.

Most clients recognize that all those non-value added activities take some time. For example, we enter the order for a repair and then wait while the order is acknowledged, scheduled, and assigned. There may be travel or setup time involved. Only then can the diagnostics be performed and the actual work accomplished. For a simple reset of equipment, the job may take only seconds but the non-value added work considerably more. For jobs that will take some time, say a few days, it's a good idea to find a temporary solution for the client and then schedule the fix. Clients invariably want to be kept abreast of the status of their jobs. They are much happier about the service when they are simply kept informed of the status, even when the job takes a long time. Knowing that, how do we structure an emergency communication vehicle that is customized to the issue and to each customer that is affected?

One company that employs this technique of continuous information is Federal Express. When an item is accepted by FedEx, the company sends a link to a website that provides continuous information about the status of the shipment. It's possible to track the item's delivery route and progress, and see a constantly updated delivery date.

In the world of partnering with customers, we want to give them reasons to continue doing business with us, reasons to value our working relationship, and fact-based information that demonstrates the value we bring. What we have done for them in the past is a matter of documented fact. All competitors can provide is a promise, a weak argument compared to our proven performance over the years.

STEP 2: EMPOWER THE ACTION TEAM WITH FULL AUTHORITY

Create a team that is committed and authorized to implement solutions that result in improved customer satisfaction. The best teams have members who are:

- Chosen for their commitment and goal orientation
- Known to have a bias for action and completion
- Team players
- Trained and educated
- Funded
- Driven by a sense of urgency
- Capable of motivating others in the organization

This group will put the problem-solving methods of Chapter 5 into practice to find the underlying causes for the problem under consideration. Once the most likely underlying cause has been identified, the empowered team can put the pilot program in place and then check to see whether the proposed solution has solved the original problem. If it has, the team will implement the changes company-wide.

Here is where many programs fail. It is easier to put change in place than it is to make changes stick for the long term. Chapter 8 will discuss methods for sustaining change. In our change implementation schemes, we should plan to:

- Update all company documentation that relates to our change
- Train operators before the change is implemented
- Review and secure buy-in for the change from the operators
- Notify vendors and customers who are affected by the change
- Set an effective date for the change to begin
- Establish auditing procedures to assure the change is implemented and effective
- Set a reward system to recognize those who are responsible for implementing and sustaining the change

Learning Organizations

When a business employs internal audits and periodic reviews to constantly improve its processes, it is on its way to becoming a learning organization.

Learning organizations share many attributes, for example a commitment to training and education for all employees. Another way an organization can show its commitment to world-class standards is by studying best practices in the industry world-wide and comparing areas for improvement to those best practices in the drive for continuous improvement. In the ISO 9001:2008 criteria, reviews are required for these and more:

- Quality management system
- Quality manual
- Process documentation
- Customer satisfaction

This is a formal and documented meeting that includes specific people in the organization. These people are on review committees that meet at regularly scheduled times during the year to review evidence that has been collected about the need for improvement in the organization. This becomes a classic case for problem-solving (as described in Chapter 5) and the use of our benchmarking or best practices comparisons. As we propose changes to our systems, we do so with an eye toward the most effective methods in the world to reset our internal processes and standards.

Assessment of Performance

Once we have a process that meets our customer's needs and it has become a part of our everyday operation, we want to assess how well it is performing.

By adding an assessment to the process, we can assure ourselves and our customers that the changes have been implemented and the benefits recognized; then we can set continuous improvement goals. If we look carefully at the rating categories, we see that high ratings on the Baldrige evaluation are attainable only by integrating quality processes into all the facets of our organization. A novice would look at the description of a program that rates a 50% to 65% Baldrige score and say that this performance is pretty good. Here is what that rating says under the "Approach" section of the rating:

> "An effective, systematic approach, responsive to the overall requirements [of the item] is evident."

This doesn't sound like a company that has mediocre performance, but to achieve a Baldrige rating of 90%–100%, here is how the approach would be described:

> "An effective, systematic approach, fully responsive to the multiple requirements [of the item] is evident."

This is a much higher level of performance, and one that must be demonstrated during the evaluation assessment.

As we establish a procedure to sustain the improvements we identified and actualized, our eyes must be on the future. Some customer needs go away and some increase in importance as competitors catch up to our lead. Some customer needs must be answered with enhanced performance to keep us "ahead of the curve." Those who stand still and revel in past accomplishments are soon taken over by the pressure of continuous competition.

In Figure 7.1 we illustrate a simple system that provides inspection for conformity at the end of the value-added processes, just prior to shipment. This final inspection minimizes the prospect of shipping bad product. However, there are negative consequences connected to waiting until the point of shipping to conduct quality inspections. Let's look at Figure 7.1.

The first disadvantage of this inspection process is that we have already added all the value into our product or service before we catch the defect. It is quite expensive to rework the product at this stage. The second disadvantage of this simple inspection process is that we will have to reconstruct the root cause of the problem in a process that may not be the same as when the rejected product was produced.

A better system is one with multiple audits and inspections. In this case we audit each process routinely to assure ourselves that the process is working as designed and as it has been documented. This preemptive approach evaluates each process at prescribed intervals as an adjunct to inspection. Then we inspect the output of each process to catch any nonconformances and correct the underlying cause as soon as the nonconformance is discovered. Catching problems at this point allows us to rework product before investing the added value of the next process. Figure 7.2 demonstrates this.

When we commit to audit and inspection throughout the system, we assure that any changes made, including those to improve customer satisfaction, will be ongoing and sustainable.

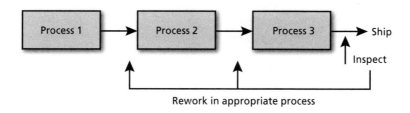

Figure 7.1   Final inspection only.

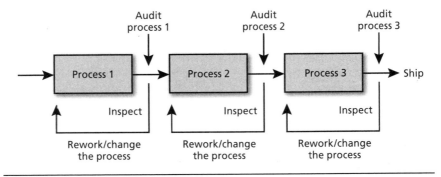

Figure 7.2 Internal audit and inspection.

As we review our processes, we must be mindful that improvement requires three things:

1. Corrective action
2. Preventive action
3. Process improvement

A process or procedure that is not in control requires *corrective action*. In this case, we know we are producing products or services that do not meet specifications and we must take immediate action to bring the process back into control. We may or may not be outside of customer specifications, but our internal quality standards should always exceed customer quality needs.

Preventive action is defined as a preemptive action to discover underlying processes that are trending out of control, have a tendency to be unstable, and have a likelihood to be out of control. Internal audits can help us find those trends and weaknesses in our processes. This is the opposite of the "fighting fires" approach of correcting something that has already gone wrong.

Internal audits are used to assure that processes are working as documented. In a certification program such as ISO 9001:2008, the internal audits are a required part of a quality process. Audit teams of employees are trained in auditing procedures and they periodically conduct audits of the company's documented processes. In this way we can catch nonconformances at the earliest stage of the process. This is a required precursor for sustainable change.

Process improvement is a commitment to continuous improvement. One might think that continuous improvement addresses only the narrow realm of product or service performance. Not so. As we reviewed earlier, continual improvement is a "must have" in all aspects of a quality system.

ISO 9001:2008 Requirements for Continual Improvement

There are many references to continual improvement in ISO 9001:2008, and they are not just for products and services. In fact, the entire management system must be reviewed at specific times throughout the year to assure that it is current with the company's practices and that it is effective. This move toward reviewing effectiveness has been a recent addition to the ISO standards. When the standards were originally envisioned, they were meant to assure consistency in output. There isn't much concern in the ISO certification process with profitability. The Baldrige criteria, on the other hand, weight *business results* as 45 percent of the score. ISO has expanded its concentration on effectiveness as distinguished from pure "compliance." For example, here are a few sections of the standard (ANSI/ISO/ASQ Q9001:2008) that specify requirements for continual improvement and effectiveness:

Paragraph 4.1: Quality Management System
"Implement actions necessary to achieve planned results and continual improvement of these processes…"

Paragraph 7.3.4: Design & Development
"…to identify any problems and propose necessary actions…"

Paragraph 8.1: Measurement, analysis, improvement
"…to continually improve the effectiveness of the Quality Management System."

Paragraph 8.2.3: "When planned results are not achieved, correction and corrective action should be taken, as appropriate."

Paragraph 8.4: "…collect and analyze data to demonstrate the suitability and effectiveness of the Quality Management System and to evaluate where continual improvement of the effectiveness of the Quality Management System can be made." This also relates specifically to the customer satisfaction data that are collected by the company.

Paragraph 8.5.2: Corrective Action
"…reviewing the effectiveness of the corrective action taken." Follow up to demonstrate that implemented improvements have achieved the effect expected.

Paragraph 8.5.3: Preventive Action
"…reviewing the effectiveness of the preventive action taken."

Although the standard doesn't specify performance on the "Business Results" category, it is clear that there is more of a concentration on the effectiveness of the system (and therefore the company) as well as on how consistent the company is in performing its tasks.

As we implement our new processes, we must be mindful of the "people" aspects of the project as well as our understanding that improvement is not a one-time deal. As soon as we implement the improvement we should be looking at the next round of study and internal evaluation that results in "continual" improvement based on comparison with world-class competitors. This is truly a journey without an end.

Note

Please see http://www.asq.org/knowledge-center/iso-9001 for more information on the ISO 9001 family of standards.

8

Sustaining the Improvements

"Quality is not an act, it is a habit."

Aristotle

In the last chapter we touched on the most important tool we have to sustain improvements, the internal audit. We have all experienced the disappointment of recommending change and implementing change, only to find that our system eventually reverted to the "old" way. What are the elements of a durable change? They are:

- Buy-in from all employees
- Internal audit (assessment)
- Reward system for achieving the new goals
- Monitoring system to quantify performance to the goals

You can't improve something that you can't measure. Neither can you monitor the improvement status of a process if you don't measure whether the changes are continuously adopted. Therefore, goals (the result we expect from our improvement efforts) should always be established in a quantitative way. Once we have set our goals for improvement, we must provide for a procedure that demonstrates success in achieving those goals. We have discussed ways to get buy-in from employees and reward them for success and we've discussed auditing and assessment of our processes. The final element we must put in place is a way to continuously monitor status in sustaining our goals. As you might imagine, this will take the form of a time-series of data where we compare current performance against the goals.

There are many ways to confirm that a process change is still in effect. One way with a strong visual impact is control charts that show the goal and current performance to the goal. This is usually updated periodically and posted for all employees, visitors, and management to see. It should be visible at the site of the process and everyone should be trained to read and interpret the chart.

Control charts are an effective way to present a continuous stream of information that shows whether a process is under control and meeting the new goals or whether it must be analyzed and adjusted.

Background for Control Charts

This chapter will concentrate on one method of tracking performance to confirm that the changes implemented are still in effect. Control charts are derived for each specific process and a detailed procedure is presented to give the reader an appreciation for this statistical approach to monitoring a repetitive process. The chapter touches on the statistical distribution of your process output, hypothesis testing to determine whether the process remains in control, the charting techniques used to initialize control charts for a sample case, and trend analysis to help you to predict whether a process is going out of control and must be adjusted before it produces unusable outputs.

Control Charts

Control charts are used to provide (continuous) assessment of processes or attributes to decide whether they are in control or whether there is reason to believe that a process is affected by a special cause of variation. If the process is acting according to statistical expectations, then we would continue the process. If the process is not meeting our expected performance, that would be a cause to study the process and determine whether there is some variation that is unexplained by our statistical expectations. In that case, we would have sufficient evidence to modify the process in order to bring it back under control.

Let's look at this in more detail. Control charts fit into the category of statistical process control tools used in the quality arena. They are used to assess repetitive processes such as manufacturing operations or service, for example collections from a call center. These are processes that occur with similar inputs and similar expected outcomes every day, week, or month. When we think about such processes, we think in terms of collecting a mean number of dollars each week or producing a specific mean bolt diameter. Certainly, every bolt coming off the line will not have that precise diameter because there will be a statistical variation coming off the machine. Similarly, the dollars collected by the call center will vary according to the nature of its process. Given this scenario, every process will have its own unique mean and variation from the mean. This is the "signature" of the process; it can't be improved unless we change the process.

If these processes are in statistical control and they follow a normal distribution, then we know the probability distribution of the parts coming off the line. It is a normal distribution as shown in Figure 8.1.

We can see that, within $+/-3$ sigma, we have captured 99.72% of all the output from our machine. In other words, of all the bolts coming off the

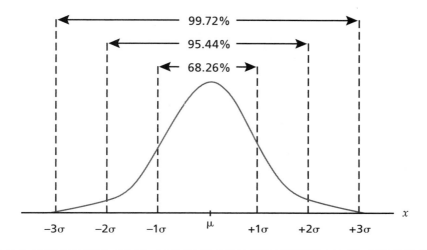

Figure 8.1 Normal distribution.

production line, 99.72% will have a diameter between +3 standard deviations from the mean and –3 standard deviations from the mean. This is the data we will use to construct our control charts. But first, let's look at an example of this process in comparison with a customer requirement for that process output. The distribution of diameters that represents the output of this process is dependent on machine tolerances and the way the machine is operated. Once purchased, adjusted, and commissioned, the machine produces bolts according to its tolerances; if maintained properly, it will do so in a sustainable manner. Let's say that this machine produces bolts that meet all our customer's requirements. Now, we sign up a new customer and the demand for tolerance is more stringent than our existing customer. This is shown in Figure 8.2.

In this figure, we have depicted a process where the new customer requirements are inside the +/–3 sigma limits. Although we were producing 99.72% of our product well within customer requirements (little scrap), our process will not meet the new customer's requirements without increasing the number of rejected bolts coming off our machines. We could satisfy both customers with the same machine. We could separate the bolts into two stacks coming off the machines and have one bin that collects only those bolts that meet our new customer requirements and another bin that contains all the rest. Then we could send to our new customer only those bolts that are made to the tighter tolerance. We have added an additional sorting step to our process, but we can use the same machine to satisfy both customers. Of course, there would have to be the right balance of orders from each customer in order to make this work. The original customer would accept any product off the machines, but the new customer would require enough

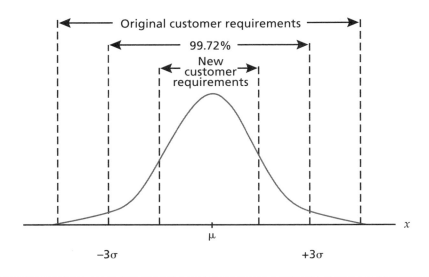

Figure 8.2 Customer requirements compared.

of the closer-tolerance products to satisfy their needs. The old customer may have shipments that include none of the close-tolerance product and the new customer will have a preponderance of close-tolerance product.

Another solution would be to improve the tolerance of the machines so that the output can meet the needs of both customers without the sorting step. That distribution would look like Figure 8.3.

This shows the machine producing the same process mean, but with a smaller standard deviation. Now, 99.72% of product falls within the new customer's specification as well, and all customers are happy with almost every part coming off the production line. Almost refers to the <0.28% (100% − 99.72%) of the product that will fall outside of customer specifications.

Now that we have an understanding of a process in statistical control, that is, one experiencing only normal variation around the mean based on the characteristics of the unique process, we can begin to understand the nature of special causes of variation.

Why would a process go out of control? Because there is a statistical distribution around all processes, we must consider a few details in order to understand the differences between normal process variation and some special causes of variation. How do we distinguish between normal statistical variation and special causes? Our goal is to leave an "in-control" process alone, and only adjust a process that we believe is out of control because of some "special" cause of variation. We will sample products and then chart their performance to see whether we are in statistical control or not. The idea is to decide whether to make a change in the process or leave it alone.

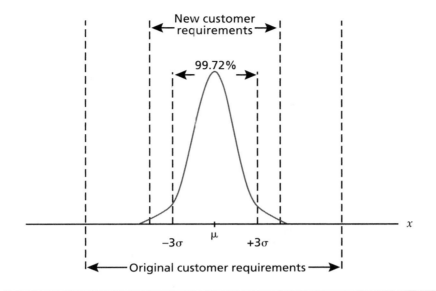

Figure 8.3   Improved machine tolerance.

Some issues to consider:

- Common causes of variation are specific to any process and can't be controlled, but they can be changed, as we did in tightening the standard deviation of the bolt diameter.
- Any process that is in control doesn't require adjustment even though all products coming off the production machines are not the same.
- Variation that is greater than that expected in a statistically controlled process is attributed to "special" or "assignable" cause.
- Special causes of variation are within our span of control and may be caused by such things as tool wear, faulty incoming material, incorrect machine settings, or operator error, to name a few.
- When confronted with a process that has a special cause of variation, we must stop the process and take corrective action to bring the process back into control.
- Just because a process is in control doesn't mean there are no special causes of variation in play. They may be too subtle for us to notice within the process of normal variation.
- If we decide to adjust a process because we have evidence that it is subject to special-cause variation, we could be wrong; even high levels of variation may come from an in-control process.

Hypothesis Testing

Let's remember that we are dealing with statistical processes. In making decisions, we must select "how right" we need to be without making a mistake. Inherent to all statistical analysis is a probability that we could be wrong. There is no such thing as complete certainty in business decision-making.

The point we make is this: "Just because a process is in-control doesn't mean there is no special-cause variation in play." We noted that, "If we decide to adjust a process…we could be wrong." Because of this uncertainty, we must carefully assess the probability of being wrong. If we could be wrong a high percentage of the time, then our monitoring is rendered useless as a business tool. Table 8.1 shows the decision process against the state of nature in our process.

Let's look at this matrix in detail. The upper left quadrant is the intersection of "Process In Control" and "Continue Process." This would be a correct decision; we would decide, after testing the process, that we would continue the process without adjustment when the process is actually in control. Similarly, in the lower right quadrant, we would adjust a process when in fact the process is not in control. This is also a correct decision. We must decide how right we want to be in assessing our decisions. Say, for instance, that we want to be right 95% of the time. (We'll see in a moment how that can be built in to our control charts.) We have accepted the probability that we could make a wrong decision 5% of the time. Now let's look at the two remaining quadrants.

The lower left quadrant says that we would decide to adjust the process when in fact it is in control. Why would we do this? Remember that "…even high levels of measurement variation may come from any in-control

Table 8.1 Decision process.

		State of nature	
		Process IN control	Process NOT in control
Our decision	Continue process	Correct decision	Type II error. False negative. Permit out-of-control process to continue. Probability = β
	Adjust the process	Type I error. False positive. Adjust a process that is in control. Probability = α	Correct decision

$\bar{x}$ chart – used for measure of control tendency for ratio data (length, time to answer a call, etc.)
R-chart – used for measure of data dispersion
UCL ⎱ When in control, there is a high probability that the sample
LCL ⎰ results are between these 2 lines.

process." If we consider the normal distribution again, we can see that the tails of the distribution go on to infinity along the *x*-axis and never quite reach a frequency of zero. Therefore, any process, even one in good control, can produce a product with a high degree of variation from the mean value. The probability of this is small, but it exists. So, we may actually have a process that is in control, with a mean that hasn't shifted, but we would conclude the process should be adjusted based on this observation. If we choose 95% probability that we would make a correct decision, then we can be wrong 5% of the time.

This is called a Type I error; t has a probability of alpha. It is also called a false positive and this probability exists in all tests. A more familiar example is the result of an EPT (early pregnancy test). There is a non-zero probability that the test says the user is pregnant when in fact she is not. This is a false positive. The same phenomenon is experienced with the PSA test that addresses men's prostate issues. There is a non-zero probability that the test shows there is a prostate problem when in fact none exists. There is a non-zero probability of a false positive error in every test, and our control charts will also be subject to this error.

The upper right quadrant is also an error possibility. In this quadrant, the process is not in control, but we can't recognize this and we continue the process. In this case, the mean of our process has actually moved, but the test sample observations are still within our expectations for statistical variation in our process. The probability of this error is beta and it represents a Type II error, also called a false negative. Using the EPT example again, the test says you are not pregnant, but in fact you are pregnant. There is a non-zero probability of a false negative occurring in every test as well.

We usually concentrate on controlling the Type I errors in our processes. When the test sample data show that the process is in control, we don't spend a lot of time trying to discern why. We save our problem-solving efforts for events that provide strong evidence that a process is out of control or trending out of control.

Why would we knowingly accept any Type I error if we have free choice to eliminate it? Why not make the alpha error 0.000000000001%? That way we'd never make a mistake in our decision to adjust a process that is really in control. What is wrong with this plan? Let's go back to our example about manufacturing bolts to demonstrate why this strategy doesn't work.

A bolt has a target diameter and a known distribution of diameters in production. Say we want the mean diameter to be 0.25 inches and we know that 99.72% of all bolts come off the production line with diameters between 0.248 inches and 0.252 inches. We know that this output is acceptable to our customers. Even if we control output so that we permit all production within this range to be considered normal variation and not subject to process adjustment, we can be wrong 0.28% of the time. This is because 99.72% of the output is between those limits, but the other .28%, *which is in control*, is product outside those limits. When we produce millions of parts, this can be a lot of scrap. In 10 million parts produced, 99.72% in-tolerance production results in 28,000 parts produced out of tolerance.

This is a good justification for taking on Six Sigma quality goals, but that is another topic. More germane to this chapter is the fact that even though we are 99.7% right, our performance is not perfect. Now, let's think about closing in our tolerance for error to 99.9999%. That would result in the production of only 10 parts per 10 million outside the tolerance range. However, to incorporate 99.9999% of all the parts in our distribution, our upper and lower limits would have to be from 0.247 to 0.253; this would increase the range by about 50%, and possibly take it outside our customer's specification. This much tolerance for product output to avoid committing a Type I error may mask a real shift in product mean that is the result of an assignable cause. In other words, we tighten up our Type I error, but increase the probability that we will commit a Type II error by continuing a process that really is not in control.

Constructing a Control Chart

With an understanding of the statistics behind process variation, we can construct a control chart for both quantitative variables and qualitative attributes.

Control Charts for Quantitative Variables (x-bar and R-charts)

A control chart is used to graphically display the results of product sampling within the context of pre-determined limits of performance. Knowing the variability of our process, we construct upper and lower control limits on a graph centered around the mean performance of our process. Let's look at an example. We will set up a control chart for a process given some accumulated data that has been collected while we know that the process is under control. This is a prime criterion for establishing control limits. If the process is not in control, then we must get it under control before we establish control limits. This makes sense because a process that is not in control has statistical variation affected by special causes that do not properly represent the stabilized capability of our process. Here is the data, in Table 8.2, which was selected because it represents a process that is in control.

The data is based on sampling the process. There are 10 samples of 5 observations per sample. We usually think of control charts as a normal distribution on its side, as shown in Figure 8.4.

Here, the +/–3 sigma limits are horizontal lines that incorporate 99.72% of all the output of our process. The mean is calculated as the mean value of all the data in all the samples. The terms we use for quantitative variables in control charts are:

k = the number of samples, in this case k = 10
n = the number of observations in each sample, in this case n = 5
x_i = each observation in all the samples
$\bar{x}_i$ = the mean of sample i as i goes from 1 to 10
$\bar{\bar{x}}$ = the mean of all the observations in all the samples
UCL = the upper control limit, calculated as $\bar{\bar{x}}$ + 3 sigma for the process
LCL = the lower control limit, calculated as $\bar{\bar{x}}$ – 3 sigma for the process

Table 8.2 A process in control.

Sample 1	Obs 1	Obs 2	Obs 3	Obs 4	Obs 5	Range	x-bar
1	3.05	3.08	3.07	3.11	3.11	0.06	3.08
2	3.13	3.07	3.05	3.10	3.10	0.08	3.09
3	3.06	3.04	3.12	3.11	3.10	0.08	3.09
4	3.09	3.08	3.09	3.09	3.07	0.02	3.08
5	3.10	3.06	3.06	3.07	3.08	0.04	3.07
6	3.08	3.10	3.13	3.03	3.06	0.10	3.08
7	3.06	3.06	3.08	3.10	3.08	0.04	3.08
8	3.11	3.08	3.07	3.07	3.07	0.04	3.08
9	3.09	3.09	3.08	3.07	3.09	0.02	3.08
10	3.06	3.11	3.07	3.09	3.07	0.05	3.08

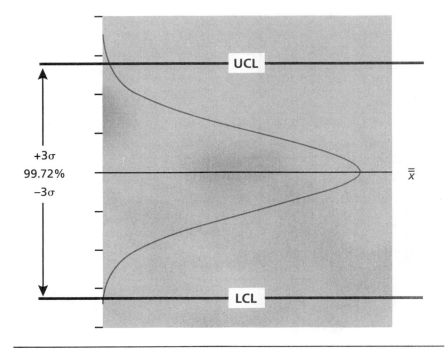

Figure 8.4 Upper and lower control limits.

However, in many cases we don't know the standard deviation of our process. The standard deviation is determined by population data over a long period of time, during which the process is tested and found to be in statistical control. This means that the process is judged to be stable and meeting the tolerances for process that were set when the process was commissioned. When that information is not available, we can substitute empirical rules for the standard deviation and use equations to calculate the upper and lower control limits. Two control charts are needed. The first chart (the $\bar{x}$ chart) plots the mean of samples collected from the process; the second is the R chart, which is the range chart of samples collected from the process. Values in the range chart are derived from the difference between the maximum value of the observations in the sample minus the minimum value of the observations in the sample. Table 8.3 shows the original data along with the calculated values of the range (maximum value minus the minimum value in each sample), and the mean of each sample ($\bar{x}_i$).

Table 8.3 Sample data for the control chart example.

Sample 1	Obs 1	Obs 2	Obs 3	Obs 4	Obs 5	Range	x-bar
1	3.05	3.08	3.07	3.11	3.11	0.06	3.08
2	3.13	3.07	3.05	3.10	3.10	0.08	3.09
3	3.06	3.04	3.12	3.11	3.10	0.08	3.09
4	3.09	3.08	3.09	3.09	3.07	0.02	3.08
5	3.10	3.06	3.06	3.07	3.08	0.04	3.07
6	3.08	3.10	3.13	3.03	3.06	0.10	3.08
7	3.06	3.06	3.08	3.10	3.08	0.04	3.08
8	3.11	3.08	3.07	3.07	3.07	0.04	3.08
9	3.09	3.09	3.08	3.07	3.09	0.02	3.08
10	3.06	3.11	3.07	3.09	3.07	0.05	3.08
					$\bar{R} =$	0.053	
					$\bar{\bar{x}} =$		3.082

for n = 5, then A2 = .577, D3 = 0, and D4 = 2.114.

The next step is to calculate the upper and lower control limits for this data without knowing the standard deviation of the process. In this case we only have sample data with no information about the underlying population. The equations for the UCL and LCL are:

For the Range Chart:
$$UCL = D_4 \times \bar{R}$$
$$LCL = D_3 \times \bar{R}$$

For the $\bar{x}$ chart:
$$UCL = \bar{\bar{x}} + A_2 \times \bar{R}$$
$$LCL = \bar{\bar{x}} - A_2 \times \bar{R}$$

Where the constants D_3, D_4, and A_2 are found in the (partial) Table 8.4, and n = number of observations per sample.

As you can see, the limits for the process come directly from our data, data that is specific to the process we are monitoring. If we know that this process is under control when we collected this data, we can check new samples in the future against these limits to see whether there has been a shift over time.

The control charts for this process are shown in Figures 8.5 and 8.6.

Time is always recorded on the x-axis. It can be scaled in time, such as 10:00 a.m., 11:00 a.m., and so on. Or it can be scaled as Sample 1, Sample 2 as we collect samples during the time period we have chosen. We want to see whether the process is still in control. Table 8.5 is a calculation sheet including a collection of samples from the process for the control chart for June 14, 2009.

Table 8.4 Abbreviated table of control chart constants.

	$\bar{x}$-chart	R-chart	
n	A_2	D_3	D_4
2	1.880	0	3.267
3	1.023	0	2.574
4	0.729	0	2.282
5	0.577	0	2.114
6	0.483	0	2.004
7	0.419	0.076	1.924
8	0.373	0.136	1.864
9	0.337	0.184	1.816
10	0.308	0.223	1.777
⋮			

114 Chapter Eight

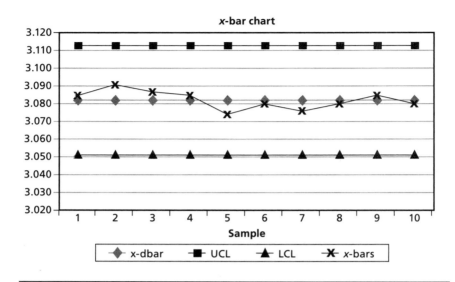

Figure 8.5 x-bar chart for the example problem.

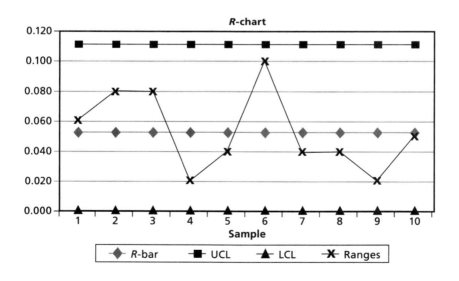

Figure 8.6 R-chart for the example problem.

A few reasons why locating your business in Nebraska increases your bottom line:

- You have your pick from a large, well-educated labor force that understands the food industry.
- You receive unbeatable business tax incentives.
- Our central location makes it easy to get to either coast.
- Electric rates 30.1% lower than the national average.

Don't forget to stop by booth N232 and pick up your free copy of our comprehensive food processing industry study. While there, enter our drawing for a chance to win Omaha Steaks.

Nebraska Public Power District

1.800.282.6773, ext. 5534
sites.nppd.com

Learn how a Nebraska location can help your business be more profitable. Stop by booth **N232** for your free copy of our comprehensive food processing industry study highlighting the Nebraska advantage.

Nebraska Public Power District

The need for two control charts is clear when we consider the definition of statistical control. We want the measure of central tendency to be consistent; equally important, we want variability to be under control as well. If we want the mean of a data set to be 5.000 and we have measured data that is 5.002, 4.999, 5.001, 5.003, 4.997, and 4.998, we can be fairly assured that there is good control around the mean. However, if we have data that is 4.000, 6.000, 3.000, 7.000, the situation is different. Although the mean of these observations is also 5.000, the variability of the observations reveals significant opportunity for out-of-specification performance in the process.

Figure 8.7 is the x-bar chart for the samples taken on that day.

Table 8.5 Sample points from inspection data.

Time of day	Obs 1	Obs 2	Obs 3	R	x	R-bar	x-dbar	UCL for R-chart	LCL for R-chart	UCL for x-bar chart	LCL for x-bar chart
10 a.m.	3.10	3.06	3.07	0.04	3.077	0.05	3.08	0.11	0.00	3.11	3.05
11 a.m.	3.11	3.09	3.05	0.06	3.083	0.05	3.08	0.11	0.00	3.11	3.05
12 p.m.	3.07	3.08	3.09	0.02	3.080	0.05	3.08	0.11	0.00	3.11	3.05
1 p.m.	3.06	3.07	3.08	0.02	3.070	0.05	3.08	0.11	0.00	3.11	3.05
2 p.m.	3.08	3.09	3.09	0.01	3.087	0.05	3.08	0.11	0.00	3.11	3.05

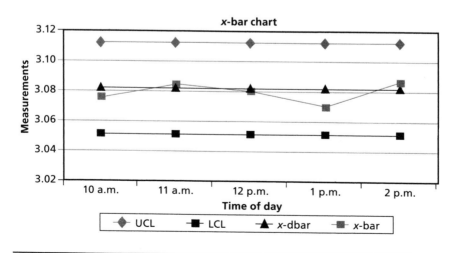

Figure 8.7 x-bar chart for the samples taken on that day.

Figure 8.8 is the R-chart for the samples taken on that day. Because none of the sample points fall below the LCL on either chart or above the UCL on either chart, we conclude that the process is still in control.

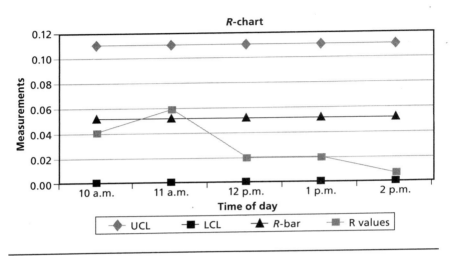

Figure 8.8 R-chart for the samples taken on that day.

Trend Analysis

The methods of control charting are very useful when looking for evidence that a process is out of control. If a sample point falls outside of our LCL or UCL limits, it is strong statistical evidence that the process is out of control and it should be adjusted. However, we can learn much more from control charts if we watch trends in performance. For instance, we know what a process looks like on a control chart if it is in control, but what does a control chart look like under different scenarios?

In Figure 8.9 we see a process that has definite sample measurements out of our control limits.

In Figure 8.10, we don't have to wait until an out-of-control condition is achieved. When there are four or five points in an increasing or decreasing pattern, we can say there is sufficient evidence to review the process for adjustment. Similarly, if the sample points are on one side of the mean or the other, we can say that a process shift has occurred. Performance indicators can be summarized as shown in the Figure 8.11.

Sustaining the Improvements **117**

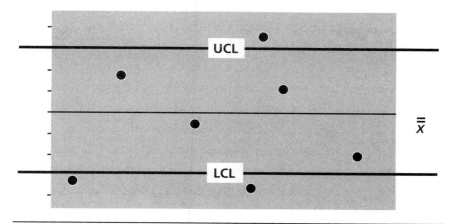

Figure 8.9 Process with sample measurements outside of the control limits.

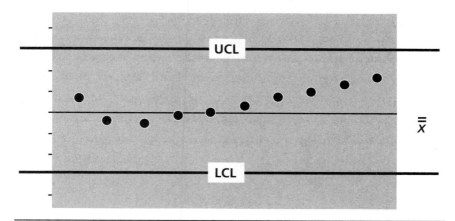

Figure 8.10 Process measurements trending out of control.

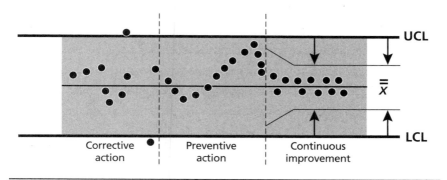

Figure 8.11 Graph of some possible outcomes in a control chart.

s-Charts

Quantitative control charts can also be developed when samples are large. Under these circumstances, we would use the standard deviation of the sample and create an "s" chart rather than using the range and creating an R chart.

Control Charts for Attributes (p-charts)

Attribute data have very simple performance criteria. A criterion is either met or unmet. Therefore, we look at attributes as a percentage or proportion meeting the requirements. This means we use a control chart called a p-chart. The most common of the p-charts is the percentage nonconforming or the percentage defective.

Readers who need more information on the methods of control charting can turn to any book on statistics or statistical process control.

Closure

This chapter is not meant as a complete treatise on control charts, but rather a single method you may use when following up on changes to your system to be assured that you are sustaining the improvements you worked so hard to achieve. The point is to show that continuously measuring compliance to your goals can help you discover when the changes you instituted are not maintained. You may then use corrective action to recover compliance to the new documented procedures.

Postscript

As we ponder the customer satisfaction dimension of our businesses, it is easy to think that there is no payout for our efforts. "You can't please all the people." Why try to improve satisfaction, when by doing so we exclude those who have different needs? If any action you take will inevitably alienate some customers, why take the chance? Why change anything and risk making things worse?

The reason is simple. We aren't pleasing all our customers today. The attempt to measure and improve customer satisfaction is aimed at increasing the population of those we satisfy and to satisfy at a higher level those who are loyal to us. By better understanding our customers' needs, we stand a greater chance of alienating fewer of them. And, in the end, since we can't satisfy all our customers, we might as well satisfy those that have more influence on our prosperity.

Not all customers are of equal value, and some customers have needs that do not coincide with our corporate direction. Successful companies focus on their core competencies and serve their specific markets extremely well, while turning away business that does not match their competencies or future plans. When properly structured, the business will be built around the needs of your good customers and not be so broad-based that it fails to meet the critical needs of any customer.

Index

Page numbers in *italics* refer to tables or illustrations.

A

analysis, dimensions of, 48–49
ANOVA (analysis of variance), 43, *43*, 47
areas needing improvement, 72–75
assessment of performance, 98–101
assignment property, *12*
attainable goals, 87
attributes
    customer-identified, 16–18
    importance of, 29, 48–49
    measuring the correct, 1–3, 42–45
average satisfaction scores, 52

B

balanced scorecard, 93–94
Baldrige Award, 95, 101
benchmarking, 18–20
biased surveys, 33
bin width, 39–41, *41*
Black Belts, 90
brainstorming technique, 61–63

C

categorization of data, 34
cause-and-effect diagram, *61*
central tendency, measures of, *14*, 34
CEO, role of, 89–90
change management, 75–81
Chi-squared probability density function, *52*
commitment stage, 77, 93–96
commuication example, *65*
communication, unscheduled, 96
competitors, 18–20, *19*
confidence intervals, 40–41
continuous improvement
    importance of, 2
    structuring the organization for, 79–81
control charts, 104–107, 110–112
    constants, *113*
    for attributes, 118
    possible outcomes, *117*
    sample data, *112*
correction factor for ties, *55*
customer communication example, 62, *65*, *66*
customer complaints, value of, 6–8, *7*
customer feedback, 25–46
customer loyalty, *28*
customer requirements, *106*, *107*
customer satisfaction
    data, 13–14
    goals, 83–92
    programs, 1–3
customer-identified attributes, 16–18
customers, past and existing, 27–28

D

data
  analyzing, 34
  gathering, 8–16
  primary versus secondary, 26
decision-making process, 70, 76, *108*
Deming process, 69
denial stage, 77
descriptive statistics, 34
dispersion, measures of, *14*
distance property, *12*
DMAIC method, 68
durable change, elements of, 103

E

early adopters, 77–78
early majority, 77–78
effective goals, characteristics of, 84–85
employee buy-in, 103
empowered teams, 97–101
equality of the means, *55*, 56
equity curve, 20–22, *21*
equity line, 22, *22*
existing customers, 28
exploration stage, 77

F

Federal Express, 96
feedback, types of, 2–3
fill-in responses, 32–33
final inspection example, *99*
first-time respondents, 48, *54*
fishbone diagram, *61*
five whys, 63–64
focused questions, 29
forced ranking scales, 11, 12
forming, of teams, 81
frequency of ratings, *13*

G

goal setting, 84–85, *85*, *86*, *87*
golfers driving distance example, 38–45, *40*, *41*
Green Belts, 90

H

histograms, 39–41
hypothesis testing, 108–110

I

importance ratings, 17–18, *19*
improvement objectives, 83–92
improvement, sustaining, 103–118
independence of samples, 50
initial non-respondents, 27, 56–58, *57*
initial respondents, 26
innovators, 77–78
inspection data, sample points from, *115*
internal audit and inspection example, *100*
interval data scales, 10–11
ISO 9001:2008 certification, 95, 101–102

K

Kruskal-Wallis one-way analysis of variance by ranks, 47–48, 50, 51, 56

L

laggards, 77–78
late majority, 77–78
leadership attributes, *80*
learning organizations, 97–98
levels of scale, *14*
lose-lose decisions, 76
low achievable goals, *85*
loyalty questions, 29
loyalty, satisfaction and, 28–29

M

machined bolts example, 104–106
mailed questionnaires, 30–31
making change happen, 88–91
management by fact, 94–95
management support, 88–90
manufacturers representatives example, 72–73

marginally achievable goals, *85*
Master Black Belts, 90
mean, 14, 35, 49–50
measureable goals, 87
measures of central tendency, *14, 35*
median, 14, 35
mnagement attributes, *80*
mode, 35

N

neutral scales, 11, 12
nominal data scales, 10–11
non-parametric analysis, 47
non-respondents, initial, 27, 48, 56–58, *57*
normal distribution, 38, *39*, 49, *105*
norming, of teams, 81
numerical data, 34
numerical responses, 32

O

objectives, setting, 88
open-ended questions, 29
order property, *12*
ordinal data metrics, 34, 35–42
ordinal data scales, 10–13, 49
origin property, *12*

P

p-charts, 118
p-value, 43
Pareto charts, 65, *66*
past customers, 27–28
performance ratings, *19*
performance, assessment of, 98–101
performance–importance analysis, *74*
performing, of teams, 81
personal interviews, 32
plan, do, study, act cycle, 64–71, *69*
preventive action, 100
primary versus secondary data, 26
probability distributions, normal, 49

problem statement: symptom, 64
process control, 106–107
process improvement, 100
process in control, *111*
process measurements trending out of control, *117*

Q

qualifying questions, 29
qualitative data, 15, *16*, 34
qualitative research methods, *9*
qualitative responses, 41–42
Quality is Free (Crosby), 91
quantitative data, 8–14
quantitative data scales, 10–14
quantitative research methods, *9, 10*
questionnaires
    formulating, 29–32
    mailed, 30–31
    organization of typical, *31*
questions, types of, 29

R

R-chart, *114, 116*
random sampling, 25–26
random variation, 49–50
range, 35–39
rank calculation for rating scores, *54, 56*
rank order analysis, 47–60
rating scores, frequency of ratings versus, *13*
ratio scales, 10–11
reaction to change, 77–78
real change, 63
realistic goals, 87
relative standing, *19*
research questions, 29–30
resistance stage, 77
resistence to change, 75–81
respondents, initial, 26
responses, types of survey, 32–33
rewards for achievement, 88, 89
Rogers Adoption/Innovation Curve, 77–78, *78*

S

sample data for control chart example, *112*
sample measurements outside of control limits, *117*
sample points from inspection data, *115*
sample size, 33–34
samples, independence of, 50
satisfaction and loyalty, 28–29
satisfaction metrics, 25–46
satisfaction ratings, 17–18
satisfaction scores, *33, 34*, 52, 53
satisfaction surveys, 33
saying "no" to customers, 72–74
scale levels and measures of central tendency, 14
scaling properties, *12*
scheduled communication, importance of, 93–94
scientific method, *67, 68*
secondary data, primary versus, 26
setting objectives, 88
Six Sigma project teams, 88
SMART goal setting, 86–87, 91
special-cause variation, 107, 108
specialty motors example, 72–74
specific goals, 87
standard deviation, 14, 35–39, *37, 44, 45*, 112
standard deviation calculation, *36*
statistical differences, 42–45
statistical process control tools, 104
statistical significance of data, 33, 49–50
statistical validity, 5–8
statistics, descriptive, 34
storming, of teams, 81
strengths, playing to, 72–75
stretch goals, *86*
sum of ranks analysis, *54, 55, 57*
survey design, *29, 30*
systems versus underlying causes, 61–64

T

teams, empowered, 97–101
telephone surveys, 31
tied observations, corrections for, 51–52, *55*
timely goals, 87
trend analysis, 116
Type I error, 109
Type II error, 110

U

underlying causes, 61–82, 63
underlying causes, systems versus, 61–64
unscheduled communication, 96
upper and lower control limits, *111*

V

value as delivery proposition, 20
variability of data, 34, 42
variation, 107
verbatim responses, 41

W

web surveys, 30–31
what customers want, 5–23
win-win decisions, 76

X

x-bar charts, 110–115, *114, 115*
x-charts, 118